WORLD
HISTORY SERIES ▪ ▪ ▪

America in the 1960s

by
Michael Kronenwetter

Lucent Books, P.O. Box 289011, San Diego, CA 92198-9011

Titles in the World History Series

America in
the 1960s

Library of Congress Cataloging-in-Publication Data

Kronenwetter, Michael.
     America in the 1960s / by Michael Kronenwetter.
          p. cm. — (World history series)
     Includes bibliographical references and index.
     Summary: Discusses a decade of enormous change and
conflict in all areas of life including science, civil rights, social
welfare, national defense, politics, and the arts.
     ISBN 1-56006-294-0 (alk. paper)
     1. United States—History—1961–1969—Juvenile literature.
[1. United States—History—1961–1969.] I. Title. II. Series.
E841.K76   1998
973.923—DC21   97–34055
                                                                      CIP
                                                                       AC

Copyright 1998 by Lucent Books, Inc., P.O. Box 289011,
San Diego, California 92198-9011

Printed in the U.S.A.

Contents

Foreword

Each year on the first day of school, nearly every history teacher faces the task of explaining why his or her students should study history. One logical answer to this question is that exploring what happened in our past explains how the things we often take for granted—our customs, ideas, and institutions—came to be. As statesman and historian Winston Churchill put it, "Every nation or group of nations has its own tale to tell. Knowledge of the trials and struggles is necessary to all who would comprehend the problems, perils, challenges, and opportunities which confront us today." Thus, a study of history puts modern ideas and institutions in perspective. For example, though the founders of the United States were talented and creative thinkers, they clearly did not invent the concept of democracy. Instead, they adapted some democratic ideas that had originated in ancient Greece and with which the Romans, the British, and others had experimented. An exploration of these cultures, then, reveals their very real connection to us through institutions that continue to shape our daily lives.

Another reason often given for studying history is the idea that lessons exist in the past from which contemporary societies can benefit and learn. This idea, although controversial, has always been an intriguing one for historians. Those who agree that society can benefit from the past often quote philosopher George Santayana's famous statement, "Those who cannot remember the past are condemned to repeat it." Historians who subscribe to Santayana's philosophy believe that, for example, studying the events that led up to the major world wars or other significant historical events would allow society to chart a different and more favorable course in the future.

Just as difficult as convincing students to realize the importance of studying history is the search for useful and interesting supplementary materials that present historical events in a context that can be easily understood. The volumes in Lucent Books' World History Series attempt to present a broad, balanced, and penetrating view of the march of history. Ancient Egypt's important wars and rulers, for example, are presented against the rich and colorful backdrop of Egyptian religious, social, and cultural developments. The series engages the reader by enhancing historical events with these cultural contexts. For example, in *Ancient Greece*, the text covers the role of women in that society. Slavery is discussed in *The Roman Empire*, as well as how slaves earned their freedom. The numerous and varied aspects of everyday life in these and other societies are explored in each volume of the series. Additionally, the series covers the major political, cultural, and philosophical ideas as the torch of civilization is passed from ancient Mesopotamia and Egypt, through Greece, Rome, Medieval Europe, and other world cultures, to the modern day.

The material in the series is formatted in a thorough, precise, and organized manner. Each volume offers the reader a comprehensive and clearly written overview of an important historical event or period. The topic under discussion is placed in a broad historical context. For example, *The Italian Renaissance* begins with a discussion of the High Middle Ages and the loss of central control that allowed certain Italian cities to develop artistically. The book ends by looking forward to the Reformation and interpreting the societal changes that grew out of the Renaissance. Thus, students are not only involved in an historical era, but also enveloped by the events leading up to that era and the events following it.

One important and unique feature in the World History Series is the primary and secondary source quotations that richly supplement each volume. These quotes are useful in a number of ways. First, they allow students access to sources they would not normally be exposed to because of the difficulty and obscurity of the original source. The quotations range from interesting anecdotes to farsighted cultural perspectives and are drawn from historical witnesses both past and present. Second, the quotes demonstrate how and where historians themselves derive their information on the past as they strive to reach a consensus on historical events. Lastly, all of the quotes are footnoted, familiarizing students with the citation process and allowing them to verify quotes and/or look up the original source if the quote piques their interest.

Finally, the books in the World History Series provide a detailed launching point for further research. Each book contains a bibliography specifically geared toward student research. A second, annotated bibliography introduces students to all the sources the author consulted when compiling the book. A chronology of important dates gives students an overview, at a glance, of the topic covered. Where applicable, a glossary of terms is included.

In short, the series is designed not only to acquaint readers with the basics of history, but also to make them aware that their lives are a part of an ongoing human saga. Perhaps they will then come to the same realization as famed historian Arnold Toynbee. In his monumental work, *A Study of History,* he wrote about becoming aware of history flowing through him in a mighty current, and of his own life "welling like a wave in the flow of this vast tide."

Important Dates in America of the 1960s

| 1960 | 1961 | 1962 | 1963 | 1964 |

1960

May 9: The Food and Drug Administration (FDA) approves use of the birth control pill in the United States.

September 26: The first televised presidential debate, between Massachusetts senator John F. Kennedy and Vice President Richard M. Nixon, is held in Chicago.

1961

January 3: The United States breaks off diplomatic relations with Cuba, beginning more than three decades of conflict with its island neighbor.

January 20: John F. Kennedy is sworn in as the thirty-fifth president.

April 12: Soviet cosmonaut Yuri Gagarin orbits the earth, becoming the first human being to travel in space.

April 17: Cuban exiles, backed by the U.S. Central Intelligence Agency (CIA), invade Cuba at the Bay of Pigs.

May 14: An integrated busload of Freedom Riders on their way to New Orleans is attacked and beaten by a white mob near Anniston, Alabama.

August 13: The Berlin Wall goes up.

1962

February 20: John H. Glenn Jr. becomes the first American to orbit the earth.

October 14: An American U2 spy plane takes pictures of Soviet nuclear missile installations in Cuba, setting off the Cuban missile crisis.

October 27: An agreement is announced ending the Cuban missile crisis: Soviets will remove their missiles from Cuba, and the United States pledges not to invade the island; some months later, U.S. missiles are removed from Turkey.

1963

August 30: In the wake of the Cuban missile crisis, the first "hot line" phone link is established between the United States and the Soviet Union allowing the leaders of the two superpowers to talk directly with each other during future crises.

November 22: Kennedy is assassinated in Dallas, Texas; Vice President Lyndon B. Johnson is sworn in to succeed him.

November 24: Accused assassin Lee Harvey Oswald is killed by Jack Ruby, ending any chance that the president's killer would explain his motives.

1964

February 11: The Beatles arrive in America to hysterical crowds.

Summer: Virtually all the major civil rights groups join forces to launch Freedom Summer—an all-out black-voter registration drive in Mississippi.

July 2: Johnson signs the Civil Rights Act, forbidding racial discrimination in hiring, in the workplace, in unions, in public accommodations, and in federally funded projects and programs.

1965

February 21: Black Muslim leader Malcolm X is gunned down in New York City.

July 30: Medicare becomes law, providing medical care for the nation's elderly.

August 11: Riots that will continue for several days break out in the Watts section of Los Angeles, California.

1967

January 27: Edward H. White Jr., Virgil I. Grissom, and Roger B. Chaffee are killed in a fire during a simulated launch of the

Apollo 1 space mission, at Cape Kennedy, Florida.

October 2: Thurgood Marshall becomes the first African American associate justice of the Supreme Court.

1968

March 16: U.S. armed forces massacre at least two hundred civilians in the Vietnamese village of My Lai.

March 31: Johnson announces that he will not run for reelection.

April 4: Dr. Martin Luther King Jr. is assassinated while standing on a balcony of the Lorraine Motel in Memphis, Tennessee.

June 5: Senator Robert F. Kennedy is assassinated immediately after winning the California Democratic presidential primary; he dies the next day.

August 29: Vice President Hubert H. Humphrey receives the Democratic

Party's nomination for president, while police and demonstrators clash on the streets of Chicago.

1969

January 20: Richard M. Nixon is sworn in as thirty-seventh president.

July 20: Neil Armstrong becomes the first human being to set foot on the moon.

August: Some 500,000 young people gather in a New York farm field to celebrate the Woodstock Music Festival.

October 15: Demonstrations, work stoppages, and other protests are held across the country as part of the Vietnam Moratorium, a national day of protest against the war.

November 15: Protesters, numbering 250,000, gather in Washington, D.C., as part of the largest single antiwar demonstration to date.

A Time of Enormous Change and Conflict

"It was the best of times, it was the worst of times."[1] When Charles Dickens wrote those words, he was talking about the age of the French Revolution, but he might have been talking about the 1960s in the United States. The decade of the sixties was a national roller coaster ride of great hope and terrible despair.

It was a time of not only idealism and enormous promise but also violent conflict and bitter disillusionment, both at home and abroad.

It was the time when the largest generation in American history grew from childhood to adulthood, and began to influence events in ways that still shape society today.

It was the time when President Lyndon B. Johnson declared "an unconditional war on poverty" and set out to build "the Great Society" in the United States.[2]

It was the time when African Americans finally freed themselves from the chains of legal segregation, as they had been freed from the chains of slavery a century before.

It was also the time of the Cold War, when the United States and the Soviet Union faced each other in angry hostility, and the peoples of both countries lived under the constant threat of nuclear annihilation.

It was the time when America finally fulfilled the ancient human dream of sending human beings to the moon.

During the 1960s many young people grew disillusioned with the ideals of previous generations and rejected mainstream American society.

It was the time when four of the most admired men in America—John F. Kennedy, Martin Luther King Jr., Robert F. Kennedy, and Malcolm X—were shot down in their primes.

It was the time when the United States fought one kind of war in Southeast Asia, and another kind of war in the streets of its own cities.

Looking back over the decade, editor William Chafe noted all these changes and succinctly encapsulated the 1960s as a time when

> Radicalism replaced moderation, a sense of [social] polarization accelerated, and the political system, so long celebrated as a source of stability in America, became a battleground where those advocating insurrection confronted others who insisted on defending the status quo and traditional values.[3]

Like the age of the French Revolution, the 1960s was a time of enormous change and conflict. To this day, many witnesses to that tumultuous decade remember it as a golden age, when America was filled with hope and promise. Others see it as a terrible time, which caused a breakdown in American society and undermined many of the nation's deepest values. From science to civil rights, from social welfare to national defense, from politics to the arts—the 1960s changed everything.

1 The Torch Is Passed

The first sign that things would be different in the sixties was the 1960 presidential election. No matter how the election turned out, it was bound to be a turning point in American history.

For one thing, the incumbent Republican president, Dwight D. Eisenhower, had been in office for eight years and could not run again. That meant that the country would begin the new decade with a new president. What was more, that president would represent a whole new generation. Eisenhower had been born in 1890, while both of the major party candidates wanting to succeed him were young enough to be his sons. No matter which man won, he would be the first president born in the twentieth century.

Like Eisenhower, both the Republican candidate, Vice President Richard M. Nixon, and the Democrat, Senator John F. Kennedy, had served in World War II. They had entered the war as lieutenants and had seen the war from a very different perspective than the men of Eisenhower's generation. But Ike, as the president was called, had begun the war as a brigadier general, and ended it as the Supreme Allied Commander. To some extent, Kennedy and Nixon saw the postwar world differently. More than most politicians of Eisenhower's generation, they looked to the future.

Overriding Questions

The United States was entering the new decade as the most prosperous nation on earth, and the leader of what Americans thought of as the "Free World"; that is, of the Western democratic nations and those Third World countries that were allied with them. The Free World, or Western bloc, was in social, economic, and military competition with the communist, or Eastern bloc, nations, which were led by the Soviet Union in Europe and communist China in Asia.

The election of 1960 revolved around two overriding questions. First, which candidate would effectively maintain American prosperity? And second, which candidate would be capable of leading the Free World in its competition with the communists?

Both candidates were committed to the free enterprise system, but each shared some of the economic attitudes of their parties. Kennedy, the Democrat, supported more government efforts to help the poor and to regulate private industry. Nixon, the Republican, wanted to rely more on private enterprise.

Both Kennedy and Nixon were Cold War warriors, committed to the struggle against international communism. In the 1950s, each had taken part, to different degrees, in controversial efforts to expose communists inside the United States.

The Candidates

The son of a wealthy and politically powerful Boston-Irish family, John Kennedy was widely considered more handsome and more charming than Richard Nixon. What is more, Kennedy was a war hero. He had single-handedly rescued an injured crewman from the ocean when the PT boat he commanded had been shot out from under them. Nixon had merely been a supply officer.

Kennedy, however, had serious disadvantages as a candidate. He was only forty-three; some people thought he was too young to be president. Then, too, he was Roman Catholic, and there had never been a Catholic president; many Protes-

tants feared that if there were a Catholic in the White House, the pope in Rome would control the administration. Kennedy and his advisers expected that his religion would lose him some votes, particularly in the Protestant South. No one knew how many votes would be lost, however, and there was always the chance that they would be canceled by Catholic Republicans who voted *for* Kennedy because of his religion. Early in the primaries, the religious issue was softened when Kennedy beat his main Democratic opponent, Senator Hubert H. Humphrey, in the heavily Protestant state of West Virginia.

Like Kennedy, Nixon had some major advantages going into the election campaign. Perhaps the most important was his governmental experience. Like the senator from Massachusetts, he had served in both the House of Representatives and Senate, but Nixon had served in the executive branch as well. He had been Eisenhower's vice president for eight years. Ike was enormously popular, and some of his

Heading into the 1960 election many Americans believed candidate Richard M. Nixon possessed the necessary political experience to make an effective president.

popularity rubbed off on Nixon. As the campaign began, it was generally believed that the better-known vice president was in the lead.

The TV Debates

The 1960 presidential campaign was the first in which television played a major role. Television had been around for many years, but until the late 1950s, relatively few American homes had sets. By 1960, however, TV had become not only an important source of news for most Americans, but also an important way in which voters assessed national candidates.

The new importance of television was underscored in 1960, when, for the first time, the major party candidates agreed to debate each other, face to face, in front of TV cameras.

There were to be four debates altogether. Almost two-thirds of the adults in the country tuned in to watch the first of the debates, more people than had ever witnessed a political event of any kind. For the first time, the nation watched mesmerized as Kennedy and Nixon debated the political issues before TV cameras carrying their words and actions to living rooms and dens across the country.

The two men stood at separate podiums, fielding questions from a panel of correspondents from ABC, CBS, NBC, and the Mutual Broadcasting Network. Political observers later concluded that what the candidates said made less of an impression than how they looked. Both candidates presented the issues well but Kennedy looked more at ease and self-assured than Nixon, who seemed tense. Nixon's persistent five o'clock shadow made him look slightly seedy on the black-and-white television screens.

Presidential candidates Richard Nixon and John Kennedy participate in one of their nationally televised debates. Kennedy, more so than Nixon, made a favorable impression on the viewing public.

Theodore H. White, who chronicled the campaign for the book he called *The Making of the President 1960,* described the viewers' reaction this way:

There was, first and above all, the crude overwhelming impression that side by side the two seemed evenly matched— and this even matching in the popular imagination was for Kennedy a major victory. Until the cameras opened on the Senator and the Vice President, Kennedy had been the boy under assault and attack by the Vice President as immature, young, inexperienced. Now, obviously, in flesh and behavior he was the Vice President's equal.[4]

Considering how close the election turned out to be, some observers believe that it was the impression the two men made in that first TV debate that gave the presidency to Kennedy.

A Close Victory

Kennedy was elected president by a total of less than 119,000 votes out of more than 68 million votes cast. A majority of white voters voted for Nixon. If African Americans had not voted overwhelmingly for the Democratic Party, Nixon would have had more popular votes than Kennedy. The same would have been true if Massachusetts had not gone heavily Democratic as well. A majority of the voters outside Kennedy's home state voted for the vice president. The popular vote was so close that some embittered Republicans grumbled that Nixon had actually won.

The presidency is not won by a total of popular votes but by votes in the Electoral College, as stipulated by the U.S. Constitution. All of a state's Electoral College votes go to the candidate who wins the most votes in that state, no matter how small the margin of victory.

The Kennedy-Nixon election hinged on close vote counts in two small districts in two large states, both of which supported the Democratic Party. One of the districts was in Chicago, where the powerful big-city mayor Richard Daley was infamous for rigging elections. The other was in rural Texas, the domain of a Democratic machine loyal to Kennedy's vice presidential running mate, Senator Lyndon B. Johnson.

If the vote in those two districts had gone Republican, the electoral votes of Illinois and Texas would have gone to Nixon— and Nixon, not Kennedy, would have won the election. Some Republicans, who knew the history of political corruption in those districts, were convinced that the election had been thrown to Kennedy. Nixon, however, refused to challenge the vote.

The New Frontier

More than anyone else, Kennedy recognized the significance of his election—and of the decade that was just getting under way. The 1950s had been a quiet decade in America, as the United States returned to normal after World War II. Eisenhower had been a caretaker president, doing little that was new or exciting.

Kennedy saw his role differently. In the past, the nation had spread west across the continent, taming the old frontier. Now, Kennedy had told the Democratic Convention that nominated him, the country was faced with a "New Frontier":

I tell you the New Frontier is here whether we seek it or not. . . . [There are] uncharted areas of science and space, unsolved problems of peace and war, unconquered pockets of ignorance and prejudice, unanswered questions of poverty and surplus.[5]

As president, it would be Kennedy's job to explore that New Frontier.

The Kennedy Image

"The torch has been passed to a new generation of Americans,"[6] Kennedy declared in his inaugural address. On a personal level, he and his family embodied that generation.

At forty-three, Kennedy was young for an American president. Only Theodore Roosevelt had been younger. Kennedy's youth was in dramatic contrast to the three presidents who came before him. Franklin Delano Roosevelt had died in office. Harry S. Truman had been in his sixties and Dwight D. Eisenhower nearly seventy when they left office.

The new president had two very young children and a young, attractive wife. He was, or at least appeared to be, extremely athletic. Eisenhower had played golf. Kennedy played touch football with his sisters, his brothers, and their wives. For many Americans, John Kennedy represented a new vigor, not just in the White House but in the country at large.

Ironically, the president was not nearly as vigorous as he seemed. In reality, his body was older, in many ways, than his age would indicate. The public did not know that he suffered from frequent periods of intense pain from a back injury.

John F. Kennedy and his wife, Jackie, symbolized a youthful vitality that seemed to reinvigorate the nation.

Despite the president's health problems, he and his wife, Jacqueline, called Jackie, brought a new spirit—a new style—to Washington. Kennedy surrounded himself with bright, inventive minds in every field of government. Many of the most knowledgeable came from the faculties of leading eastern universities, especially Harvard, where Kennedy had studied.

Kennedy believed in the power of the presidency to set an example for the nation, and he made the White House a center of culture. He let it be known that he was a voracious reader; he took every opportunity to show his admiration for serious artists. He invited the poet Robert Frost to read one of his poems at his inauguration. Frost wrote a new poem for the occasion.

Kennedy's Inaugural Address

John F. Kennedy was inaugurated as the thirty-fifth president of the United States on January 20, 1961. It was a cold, blustery day in Washington, D.C. Some saw the rough weather as an ill omen, signaling stormy times ahead. Others saw the brisk wind as bracing: a fit environment for a vigorous new administration.

The speech Kennedy gave that day—excerpted here from Louis Filler's The President Speaks: From William McKinley to Lyndon B. Johnson—*is one of the most memorable inaugural addresses in history. It ushered in not only a new administration but a new era in American history.*

"We observe today not a victory of party but a celebration of freedom, symbolizing an end as well as a beginning, signifying renewal as well as change. . . .

The world is very different now. For man holds in his mortal hands the power to abolish all forms of human poverty and all forms of human life. And yet the same revolutionary belief for which our forebears fought is still at issue around the globe, the belief that the rights of man come not from the generosity of the state but from the hand of God. . . .

Let the word go forth from this time and place, to friend and foe alike, that the torch has been passed to a new generation of Americans, born in this century, tempered by war, disciplined by a hard and bitter peace, proud of our ancient heritage, and unwilling to witness or permit the slow undoing of those human rights to which this nation has always been committed, and to which we are committed today at home and around the world.

Let every nation know, whether it wishes us well or ill, that we shall pay any price, bear any burden, meet any hardship, support any friend, oppose any foe to assure the survival and the success of liberty.

This much we pledge—and more. . . .

Finally, to those nations who would make themselves our adversary, we offer not a pledge but a request; that both sides begin anew the quest for peace, before the dark powers of destruction unleashed by science engulf all humanity in planned or accidental self-destruction. . . .

All this will not be finished in the first one hundred days. Nor will it be finished in the first one thousand days, nor in the life of this Administration, nor even perhaps in our lifetime on this planet. But let us begin. . . .

And so, my fellow Americans, ask not what your country can do for you; ask what you can do for your country."

Once in office, Kennedy invited every kind of performing artist to the White House. On one memorable occasion, a Shakespeare company, a ballet company, the actor Frederick March, and the great cellist Pablo Casals, violinist Isaac Stern, and composer Igor Stravinsky all performed in the White House East Room on the same evening.

Policies

Kennedy wanted his administration to be as vigorous as his own public image. In the first two years of his administration, he launched a barrage of new initiatives in foreign and domestic policies alike.

While continuing to build up the U.S. military, to protect the country against its enemies, Kennedy took measures to shore up relations with America's friends. Among those measures was the Alliance for Progress, a series of economic agreements designed to assist economic and social development in Latin American countries.

The most characteristic of Kennedy's foreign policy proposals was the Peace Corps. This new government agency asked talented Americans from various walks of life to donate two years of their time to promote international peace by doing public service in foreign countries. Most, although not all, of the Americans who enlisted in the Peace Corps were young.

Domestically, the New Frontier looked like a new version of Roosevelt's New Deal. The president proposed a host of social and economic initiatives. They included raises in the minimum wage and Social Security benefits, new programs to aid the nation's schools, long-range plans to foster conservation, and guidelines to promote urban development.

Congress, however, was dominated by an alliance of conservative Democrats and Republicans who considered many of these programs both too liberal and too expensive. Although Congress did approve an increase in Social Security benefits and a massive urban development program, it turned down proposals to provide federal aid to schools and medical care for the elderly.

Managing the Economy

Although many of Kennedy's proposals were considered liberal, his economic goals were surprisingly conservative. He believed in balancing the federal budget and keeping inflation low.

Kennedy was an activist president who used the power and prestige of his office to promote his economic goals—even when that meant putting pressure on his political allies. Among those allies were the big unions who traditionally supported the Democrats. In 1962, Kennedy persuaded the United Steel Workers to moderate its salary demands in negotiations with the big steel companies. He was afraid that much higher wages for steelworkers would signal higher steel prices and a new round of inflationary labor contracts.

Although the union went along with the president's request, several of the biggest steel companies refused to match their workers' restraint. Despite the union's concessions, they went ahead and announced a big rise in steel prices.

The president was outraged. He publicly attacked the steel companies, and let it be known he was looking into taking antitrust legal action against them. He set out to deny them some of their profits by instructing federal agencies to order steel only from companies that had not raised their prices.

Kennedy's actions in the steel crisis showed the nation that the young president could be tough when it was demanded of him. At the same time, those actions earned Kennedy the distrust of powerful big business interests and their allies in Congress.

In most respects, the economy did well under Kennedy's management. Unemploy-

A Peace Corps volunteer in Nigeria. The Peace Corps attracted many young idealists who wished to donate their time to help developing nations.

ment, however, stayed stubbornly high at over 5 percent of the workforce. That is considered more or less normal by today's standards, but it was widely considered alarming in the early 1960s. Kennedy's solution was a big tax cut, which he hoped would encourage businesses to expand and employ more people.

John F. Kennedy would not live to see the result of his tax cut. Nor would he live to see the end of the decade his election had ushered in.

"We'll Never Be Young Again"

On November 22, 1963, President Kennedy paid a political visit to Dallas, Texas. He was up for reelection in 1964, and Texas was going to be a vital part of his campaign strategy. The Texas Democratic Party was in upheaval, and the president hoped that his trip there might mend some political fences.

Riding in an open car through the Dallas streets, waving to the crowd, the president was shot by a sniper from an upstairs window in the Texas School Book Depository building. Jackie Kennedy, who was sitting next to her husband when the bullet hit, was spattered with his blood. John Connally, the governor of Texas, who was riding in the president's car, was seriously wounded.

In that moment of terrible violence, America's sense of itself—and the promise of the future—was shattered. People who heard the news were not only shocked but dazed. Such things could not happen in the United States, they told themselves.

Not in the bright new decade of the 1960s, not when the country was doing so well. True, other presidents had been shot before, but never one so young, so vital, so full of life. It couldn't be true.

But it was true. The president was dead. With him, some part of the hope and optimism that he had symbolized for the entire country was dashed.

There would be three presidents in the 1960s. The others would serve much longer than John Kennedy, and, by most standards, they would achieve much more. And yet it is Kennedy who is by far the most admired—and the best loved—of the three presidents in that decade.

People still speak of his few short years in office as America's Camelot. The com-

A Country Grieves

William Manchester wrote an admiring book about John Kennedy called Portrait of a President, *which explored his early years in office. Five years later—four years after the president had been assassinated in Dallas—Manchester wrote an epilogue for a new edition of that book in which he tried to explain what the country had lost.*

"Those whose job it is to study Presidents had written that he was too remote from the people, too lacking in folksy charm. Then he was dead and a million lined the streets of Washington to watch the gun carriage bearing his body pass. The entire world went through a convulsion of grief. And why? Because of his elegance, his self-deprecating wit, his sophistication? That was largely camouflage. . . .

He wrote of valor, believed in heroes, and made his life a monument to that faith. Duty, dedication, and devotion lay at the core of him, and if those words sound quaint, the fault lies with us and not with them. 'Unless democracy can produce able leaders,' he had written at Harvard, 'its chances of survival are slight.' That thought became his keel . . . he wasn't even especially tall. But he appeared taller because he was reaching, and because he would never stop reaching his grasp became quite extraordinary."

John F. Kennedy's death sent the nation into mourning, but his popularity would outlast his term in office.

John F. Kennedy's motorcade passes by crowds on a Dallas street. Minutes later the president would be struck by an assassin's bullet.

parison refers to the glorious period of progress and chivalry that was said to exist in ancient Britain under the rule of King Arthur—a period that, like the life of John F. Kennedy, was sadly short.

To this day, most Americans who were alive in 1963 remember where they were and what they were doing when they heard of the assassination. To many of them—particularly those who were young at the time—the president represented not only a country and a generation, but also the promise of a boundless future. According to William Manchester, Kennedy's friend:

No matter where we had been on November 22, millions of us had suffered an irreparable loss when word came that John Kennedy had been killed. We would never again be completely whole; when we went to Arlington [National Cemetery] we knelt by the grave of the selves we had been. [U.S. senator Daniel] Pat Moynihan had put it superbly the evening after the tragedy. "We'll never laugh again," [syndicated columnist] Mary McGrory had told him. "Oh, we'll laugh again," Pat had said. "But we'll never be young again."[7]

2 Growing Up in the 1960s

When President Kennedy declared that the torch had been passed to a new generation of Americans in 1961, he was only half right. In reality, the torch had been passed to *two* new generations.

The first was Kennedy's own generation, the men—and they were all men—who were taking over positions of leadership from the senior men who had seen the country through the Great Depression and World War II. But there was another, even younger generation, who would put its stamp on the 1960s every bit as dramatically as Kennedy's would.

They were the first of the so-called baby boomers: the Americans born between the mid-1940s and the early 1960s, many of them the children of servicemen back from World War II. They would make up the largest generation in the history of the United States; they would dominate the vast cultural changes that took place in the 1960s, and for decades to come.

America in 1960

It is hard for those who have grown up since the 1960s to understand how different life in America was when that decade began. The 1960s marked so many drastic changes in

the American lifestyle that the United States of the late 1990s might seem like another country to a time traveler from 1960. Charles Murray and Catherine Bly Cox explain:

> In the first year of John Kennedy's administration, the country was in transition between Eisenhower's fifties and the years that would be remembered as The Sixties. In movie theaters, the hits still tended to be big stories with big stars playing good guys. . . . Popular music was still Elvis Presley and Connie Francis, the Marcels and the Shirelles—it would be more than two years before the Beatles had their first hit. Prices were still fifties-style too: *The Washington Post* . . . informed its readers that they could buy porterhouse steak for seventy-nine cents a pound at the A&P or a four-bedroom house in fashionable Chevy Chase for a price in the "mid-20s." As for unrest on the campuses, there was indeed a loud, disruptive demonstration at Harvard that spring—but it was to protest the substitution of English for the traditional Latin on diplomas.[8]

Nothing that can be said about life in a country as big and diverse as the United States can ever be true for everyone. For the most part, though, middle-class Americans dressed, looked, and saw themselves very differently when the 1960s began than they do today. Men wore suits, ties, and hats to baseball and football games. Males of all ages wore their hair short. If a man's hair was not trimmed to a crew cut stubble, it was plastered down with hair cream—or even Vaseline. Facial hair was considered shocking on a teenage boy. Even on a mature man, all facial hair except for a mustache was considered eccentric in most parts of the United States.

Females of all ages spent hours combing their hair into elaborate styles that were difficult to maintain. Often their hair appeared cemented in place with a combination of hairspray, barrettes, and bobby pins. In Christian churches, the women wore hats and gloves. Even the thinnest teenage girl wore a girdle under her clothing, and garter belts were commonplace.

For a male to use a four-letter word in the presence of a woman was considered improper, and sometimes downright shocking. For an adult to use such a word in front of a young person was considered shameful. For a teenage girl to use a four-letter word in any company was considered disgraceful.

Americans could not vote until they were twenty-one years old. Young people were expected to respect authority. In most families, teenagers who spoke back to their parents or showed them open disrespect could expect to be severely punished. Birth control information was unavailable to teenagers. Condoms were sold only in drugstores. Even there, they were kept under the counter and out of sight. They had to be asked for.

In many states, adultery or desertion was virtually the only grounds for a legal divorce. Abortion was illegal.

Even outside the South, whites and blacks were kept apart, whether by law or rigid custom. African Americans were not expected to associate with whites, except on the job, where, in most cases, they would have white bosses. Very few black employers had white employees.

Most young people were raised in the belief that their highest ambition should be to get a good job, with a good company, and spend the rest of their working lives there.

Americans of all ages and ethnic backgrounds tended to trust their government, although not necessarily all the politicians

Although the mid-to-late sixties spawned a liberation of fashion, hairstyles, and social attitudes, the majority of Americans remained conservative in their appearance and way of life.

who ran the government. Most people assumed that the U.S. government had their best interests at heart; they believed that what the government told them must be true. When critics accused the government of lying to the public about what it was doing in countries like Vietnam or Cuba, most people dismissed the critics as communists or wild-eyed paranoids.

By the end of the 1960s, many of these things would be changed; the rest were well on their way to changing.

"What whirlwind smashed the idyllic world of the '50s?" writer Garry Wills would ask, more than thirty years later:

> The campuses with their . . . dress codes, the family with its "togetherness" and propriety, the churches with their patriotism and fund raising, the corporations with their grey suits and keys to the executive bathrooms? . . .
>
> A confluence of many forces was at work. The serenity of the Eisenhower years, and the excitement of the Kennedy years rode an unparalleled surge of prosperity . . . a youth culture, based on expensive tastes, has become a key factor in the economy. There was room, it was felt, for both idealism and hedonism. . . . Doing good and having a good time seemed natural partners. . . . Optimism was running high.[9]

Pride and Prosperity

The United States was incredibly proud and prosperous as it entered the 1960s. Unlike its allies and enemies in World War II, it had survived the war intact, to become unquestionably the richest and most powerful country in the world. In the years since, it had built the biggest and strongest economy the world had ever known, and the majority of Americans were enjoying the fruits of that economy.

There were still large areas of poverty in the midst of all this plenty, but most middle-class and upper-class Americans were hardly aware of them. For those lucky Americans, life was more comfortable and more secure than for any people in the history of the world. This economic prosperity would continue throughout the decade. There would be ups and downs, but, overall, the 1960s would be the most prosperous decade in American history.

The generation of middle-class Americans who came of age in the 1960s took this prosperity for granted. What is more, they were raised to assume that the United States was not only the wealthiest and most powerful nation in the world, but that it was also the most noble. The United States, they were taught, had won two world wars against tyranny, and was now the leader of the Free World. The United States stood for freedom and equality, both at home and around the world.

The Beginning of Disillusionment

About the time they were in high school, however, many young Americans began to question whether that image was really accurate. For them, as one disillusioned young American declared:

> The declaration "all men are created equal . . ." rang hollow before the facts of Negro life in the South and the big

What Made Them Different?

The generation that came of age in the late 1940s and 1950s had been called "the silent generation." They were ambitious and hardworking, but not very socially or politically active. The generation that came of age in the 1960s would become more active in social and political causes than virtually any American generation that had come before it.

What made them different? Some answers to that question were given in the Port Huron Statement, a 1962 manifesto of the radical leftist organization Students for a Democratic Society (SDS), written by young activist Tom Hayden and published in Vandals in the Bomb Factory.

"We are people of this generation, bred in at least modest comfort, housed now in universities, looking uncomfortably to the world we inherit.

When we were kids the United States was the wealthiest and strongest country in the world; the only one with the atom bomb, the least scarred by modern war, an initiator of the United Nations that we thought would distribute Western influence throughout the world. Freedom and equality for each individual, government of, by, and for the people—these American values we found good, principles by which we could live as men. Many of us began maturing in complacency.

As we grew, however, our comfort was penetrated by events too troubling to dismiss. First, the permeating and victimizing fact of human degradation, symbolized by the Southern struggle against racial bigotry, compelled most of us from silence to activism. Second, the enclosing fact of the Cold War, symbolized by the presence of the Bomb, brought awareness that we ourselves, and our friends, and millions of abstract 'others' we knew more directly because of our common peril, might die at any time. We might deliberately ignore, or avoid, or fail to feel all other human problems, but not these two, for these were too immediate and crushing in their impact. . . .

Some would have us believe that Americans feel contentment amidst prosperity—but might it not better be called a glaze above deeply-felt anxieties about their role in the new world? And if these anxieties produce a developed indifference to human affairs, do they not as well produce a yearning to believe there is an alternative to the present, that something can be done to change circumstances in the schools, the workplaces, the bureaucracies, the government? It is to this latter yearning, at once the spark and engine of change, that we direct our present appeal."

College campuses became forums for social protest and political debate during the 1960s. The constant discussion of issues kept people interested in politics and often showed the power of political organization.

cities of the North. The proclaimed peaceful intentions of the United States contradicted its economic and military investments in the Cold War status quo.[10]

Faced with this conflict between what they had been taught and what they saw in the real world around them, many young Americans began to question everything they had been taught. Among the things they questioned were the values of their parents' generation. Maybe getting a good job, and a car, and a house in the suburbs was not so important after all.

Some young people looked for greater meaning in political causes. College campuses became hotbeds of political activity, with groups like the left-wing Students for a Democratic Society (SDS) stirring up hostility toward the Establishment that it blamed for much that was wrong with America. Students in the 1960s demonstrated in support of all sorts of causes: from civil rights to peace in Vietnam; from an end to the military draft to the legalization of marijuana; from the right of

students to set their own curriculums to a demand for coed dorms.

At the University of California at Berkeley, the so-called Free Speech movement even demanded the right to shout four-letter words in public—something that shocked even many political radicals.

Meanwhile, many "straights," who were opposed to the drug culture, reacted to the left-wing radicalism of SDS and the Free Speech movement by joining right-wing groups like the Young Republicans or John Birch Society.

The Hippies and the Counterculture

Some young Americans rejected traditional American culture altogether. They attempted to create a new culture of their own. Instead of being competitive, like traditional American society, this culture—or counterculture—would be based on sharing and mutual respect. The new hippie culture, as it was called, was based on the ideals of peace, love, and brotherhood. According to author William O'Neill, "Hippies lived together in 'tribes' or 'families.' Their golden rule was 'Be nice to others, even when provoked, and they will be nice to you.'"[11]

The obvious outward indications of membership in the counterculture were long hair, beards, and colorful clothing. The chief emblems were the peace signs: the drawn symbol of an upside-down Y inside a circle, and the physical gesture made by extending the first two fingers in a V.

As described by sociologist Harry Silverstein, the hippies were "predominantly middle class."

[T]hey are not necessarily clear about their goals. Except perhaps, for one: they don't like that which they've experienced in the communities in which they've been reared, and thus you have a repudiation of the society in which they have been socialized. They come . . . looking for something else. Sometimes it's called experience, another way of life, love, greater freedom, more individuality. But it's not goal-oriented in the sense of the middle class. It's simply a withdrawal from a kind of community they don't particularly like.[12]

Hippies delighted in "freaking out"— an expression of the time—the middle class they rejected by flaunting the more shocking aspects of their lifestyles, particularly psychedelic drugs and sexual liberation.

"You want to know what a hippie is?" asked a sly member of the rock group the Fugs. "A hippie is a young person who older people in authority feel is having more fun than they think he should be having. That's what a hippie is."[13]

There were hippie communes (communities in which everyone shared what-

ever they had) all over the country. The geographic center of the counterculture, however, was the Haight-Ashbury neighborhood of San Francisco. Its nickname of the Haight (pronounced hate) was an ironic one for a place in which to build a culture based on love.

For a time in the mid-1960s, young Americans from all over the country flocked to the Haight to find freedom, and to experiment with new values and new lifestyles. Some older Americans came there, too. According to one local store owner:

The place was swarming with all kinds of people. People with minks on, people with long hair, a kid with Indian clothes and a beard. It was America

The Haight-Ashbury district of San Francisco attracted both young and old social dropouts who were looking for new cultural values and acceptance of their eclectic lifestyles.

coming into that store, for some reason. It looked to me like the start of something good.[14]

It looked that way to a lot of people, including Wes Wilson, the artist responsible for many of the psychedelic-style posters so typical of the time:

I think the hippies are sort of like the beginning of something which is going to be different. I think there will probably be very few people in the Haight-Ashbury who will go into a very disciplined scene. . . . I don't think the system we're living in is going to outlast the hippies. The system will change. The thing that's happening with hippies is a growth, not a static thing. And so, it's like saying, "How long will this new principle be in action?" I would

Hippies experimented with various forms of self-expression, including the donning of brightly colored and often outrageous clothing.

say that most of the young people in this country, in ten years or sooner, will be of this kind of morality and system.[15]

The hippies believed in the freedom to do whatever one wanted to do, so long as it did not harm anyone else. Most especially, many believed in "expanding their consciousness" with drugs. According to William O'Neill:

Drugs were important [to the counterculture] both as a means to truth and advancers of the pleasure principle. . . . [The Haight] became the first community in the world to revolve entirely around the buying and selling and taking of drugs.[16]

Drugs were not only at the heart of the hippie experience, but also became like an infectious disease. Among their victims were many of the very young and vulnerable who flocked to the Haight, looking for love, only to find exploitation. One hippie described a familiar occurrence there:

Pretty little 16-year old middle class chick comes to the Haight to see what it's all about. [She] gets picked up by a 17-year old street dealer who spends all day shooting her full of speed again & again . . . & raffles off her temporarily unemployed body for the biggest Haight Street gang bang since the night before last.[17]

Divided Generations

The generation that grew up in the 1960s was famous for its rebellion against traditional American values. It was during the 1960s that the phrase "the generation gap" came into use to describe the stark differences in the opinions and attitudes of young people and their parents. But not all young people rebelled. In fact, only a minority actually took drugs regularly, joined communes, or took part in demonstrations, whether in favor of the civil rights movement or against the Vietnam War.

Many young people of the time shared the values of their parents' generation and lived the kind of lives their parents hoped for them. They were every bit as ambitious, conservative, and competitive as their parents. These young Americans not only despised the hippies, but thought that the peaceniks, who called for an end to the Vietnam War, were traitors. These straights—as they were called—rejected drugs and considered all sex outside of marriage immoral.

Even among those who did rebel—whether with drugs, sex, or politics—there were many divisions. Most hippies were not political at all, and many left-wing activists were personally uncomfortable with drugs. Even those who made up what was called the Movement—the conglomeration of organizations and people who acted to oppose racial and economic oppression and the Vietnam War—disagreed about all sorts of things.

The most radical followers of the New Left preached violent revolution against the wealthy power structure they believed was oppressing the nation. The American Friends Service Committee, which counseled young men who wanted to keep out of the military draft, was determinedly pacifist. The Yippies (Youth International Party) were as interested in stirring up mischief and having fun as in any serious political cause. The term *Yippies* also stood for a traditional cheer of celebration.

"Never trust anyone over thirty" was a common expression among the young rebels of the 1960s. Feeling that they had been misled by their parents' generation, they were determined not to be deceived again. However, the truth is that the cultural and political controversies of the time never divided neatly along generational lines.

Senior Sympathy

Not all young people joined the Movement, and not all members of earlier generations rejected it. Some seniors supported at least some of the radical positions taken by the young. Among them was Dr. Benjamin Spock, the famous pediatrician who had written *Baby and Child Care*, the book that millions of American parents had used for guidance in how to raise their children. Spock—born in 1903—joined with many of those same children in demonstrating against the Vietnam War. He was sentenced to two years in prison for advising some of them to evade the military draft.

It was also an older generation that produced Dr. Timothy Leary. A Harvard professor, born in 1920, Leary preached the power of LSD to "expand consciousness." He became famous for counseling young people to "turn on, tune in, and drop out." That is, to "turn on" with drugs, "tune in" to the insights that drugs supposedly inspired, and "drop out" of traditional American society.

Spock and Leary were extreme examples of senior Americans who sympathized with the rebellious young. But there were many ordinary adults who shared their distaste for hypocrisy and for the Vietnam

Harvard professor Timothy Leary advocated the use of hallucinogenic drugs to reach "expanded" states of consciousness.

War. There were also many parents who actually admired their children's idealism and respected their courage in rejecting traditional values, even when they did not share their views.

The Birth of a Sexual Revolution

The counterculture was almost as sexist as traditional American society. For the most part, young men tended to lead and make the decisions, and young women were expected to follow. In most communes, where several people of both sexes lived together in small, self-invented societies, it was the women who were expected to do the housekeeping chores. Even in the Movement, where everyone talked a lot about individual freedom and equality, virtually all the leaders were men.

Even so, it was from the events of the 1960s that the feminist movement, which would only flower in the 1970s, would spring. Young women, imbued with the ideals of personal and political freedom that swirled around the Movement, began to question their roles, not just in society but in the counterculture itself.

The modern feminist movement may have begun with the publication of Betty Friedan's landmark book, *The Feminine Mystique*, in 1963. Friedan was also a founder of NOW (the National Organization for Women), the most influential of the feminist groups founded in the 1960s.

More radical groups with names like SCUM (Society for Cutting Up Men) and WITCH (Women's International Conspiracy from Hell) grabbed public attention with stunts like burning bras in public and picketing the Miss America contest with signs proclaiming Miss America Sells It. Some of the most radical declared that men were the source of all evil and that women should refuse to have anything to do with them.

However, the most significant event in the long-term development of the modern women's movement was not political at all. It was medical. In 1960, the federal Food and Drug Administration (FDA) approved the use of a birth control pill. For the first time, women had an effective method of birth control that they could use themselves, without depending on men to cooperate.

Until then, the fear of pregnancy had acted as a powerful deterrent to sexual activity for most young women. Many of them now felt freed from sexual restraint. The ultimate result of the pill—combined with the ideals of personal freedom and adventure that flourished in the counterculture—would be the so-called sexual revolution that transformed sexual habits in the 1960s.

Rock 'n' Roll

Music was vital to the generation that came of age in the 1960s. Rock 'n' roll had begun in the 1950s when they were children, and they had been raised to respond to the rhythms of Elvis Presley, Bill Haley and the Comets, Jerry Lee Lewis, Buddy Holly, and Fats Domino.

Most parents didn't know what to make of the new music. For the teens of the 1960s, rock 'n' roll seemed like a form of rebellion. It was not a coincidence that the first big rock 'n' roll hit—Bill Haley's "Rock Around the Clock"—was the featured song in the movie *The Blackboard Jungle*, which dealt with juvenile delinquents.

Virtually all young people—straights, political radicals, and hippies alike—embraced at least some form of rock music. The straights tended to favor the likes of Chuck Berry, the surfer songs of the Beach Boys, or the equally noncontroversial Motown groups. Political types favored protest singers like Joan Baez, Phil Ochs, and Bob Dylan; they began to cross the line between folk and rock in 1965.

The hippies indulged in music related to the drug scene or drug experiences, such as songs by the Grateful Dead and the Jefferson Airplane. For them, as Chester Anderson wrote in the hippie newspaper *San Francisco Oracle:*

> Far from being degenerate or decadent, rock is regenerative & revolutionary art, offering us our first real hope for the future (indeed for the present) since August 6, 1945 [the day the atomic bomb was dropped on Hiroshima, Japan] . . . rock is a way of life, international & verging in this decade on universal . . . rock constitutes what might be called a 20th Century magic.[18]

Radical women's groups protested the social constraints they endured during the 1960s. Here, a group of activists relinquish their bras to symbolically demonstrate the removal of gender restrictions.

Not everyone took rock 'n' roll that seriously, but almost everyone enjoyed it. There was a lot of crossover. A few groups, like the Beatles—whose music ranged from the cheerful mindlessness of "Help!" and "I Want to Hold Your Hand" to the psychedelic meanderings of the *Sgt. Pepper's Lonely Hearts Club Band* album—were popular with almost everyone.

Hippies sit atop their psychedelically painted van during the 1969 Woodstock Music and Art Festival, a three-day concert that reflected the peaceful creed of the hippie movement.

Woodstock

Considering the importance of music to the whole 1960s scene, it is fitting that the decade reached a kind of symbolic climax with a music festival. The Woodstock Music and Art Festival, which was held on a farm in upstate New York on a rainy weekend, became an instant watershed.

On August 15, 1969, some 500,000 young people—hippies, political radicals, and straights alike—gathered together to celebrate rock 'n' roll, youth, and the freedom to enjoy them both. Among the performers were Jimi Hendrix, Richie Havens, the Grateful Dead, Janis Joplin, the Jefferson Airplane, and the Who.

Several of the spectators took off their clothes. Some "dropped acid"—the most popular psychedelic drug of the era—and lost themselves in drug-induced fantasies, some pleasant and some nightmarish. Many smoked pot. The police stayed away; the weekend stayed peaceful.

Even when the rain poured down mercilessly—soaking everyone and turning the farm fields to mud—no one seemed to care. Another generation of participants might have fled for cover, but not the young people at Woodstock. The performers simply continued to play their electric instruments, risking electrocution from lightning, while the spectators frolicked in the mud.

The Woodstock Music Festival was not only the largest music festival the world had ever seen, but also an enormous self-affirmation of the generation that had come of age in the 1960s: a testament to their spirit and their exuberance—the ultimate demonstration that they had arrived, and were a force to be reckoned with.

Chapter

3 The Cold War

The end of World War II had left two superpowers in the world: the United States and the Soviet Union. They saw each other not only as competitors but also as ideological enemies. The United States saw itself as the defender of the Free World—the standard-bearer of representative government and the free enterprise system. In contrast, the Soviet Union proclaimed itself the standard-bearer of communism—an economic and political system overtly opposed to capitalism and the class divisions of the West.

Both sides saw their ideals—and their positions in the world—as incompatible. The Soviets believed that the people of the Western nations should revolt and throw off the governments and capitalist corporations that dominated them. The United States supported those governments and corporations.

This state of political and military tension was known as the Cold War. It was not a "hot" war in which the two sides were actively fighting each other. On the other hand, it was not peace, either. Instead, the two sides faced each other in mutual hostility, prepared for, and half-expecting, a hot war to break out at any moment.

Many people on both sides felt that an ultimate conflict between the two superpowers was inevitable. Two sides so opposed to each other could not coexist forever. Sooner or later, one must defeat the other. The great fear was that the final conflict, when it came, might be carried out with nuclear weapons.

The Arms Race

The decades following World War II saw a massive arms race between the United States and the Soviet Union. Each superpower feared that the other might attack at any time. Richard Nixon expressed the general belief of most Americans of both parties as the country entered the 1960s:

> There is no question but that the first consideration which must motivate any Administration is national survival. The United States must do what is necessary to maintain an adequate military posture: regardless of what any potential enemy of the United States may have, if that enemy should launch an attack, we must be able to retaliate and to destroy its war-making potential.[19]

The result of this mutual determination was a desperate race to build more powerful weapons. The stage for this arms race had been set by two developments

The 1960s were laced with fear of atomic annihilation. Both the United States and the USSR had stockpiled enough nuclear warheads to ensure mutual destruction in the event of war.

that occurred near the end of World War II. The first was the Nazi advances in the field of rocketry. German scientists had produced two generations of unmanned rockets—the V-1s and the V-2s—with which Germany had attacked England from across the English Channel. The second development was the production, in the United States, of the atomic bombs that had been dropped on Japan at the end of World War II.

The combination of missiles that could travel from one country to another and atomic explosives that could blow up an entire city was enough to tempt both superpowers. It was also enough to terrify them.

Following the war, both sides launched projects to build more powerful rockets. It was not long before more missiles were being manufactured that could carry nuclear warheads from the United States to the Soviet Union, and vice versa. At the same time, new generations of atomic weapons were being developed that could be carried by these missiles. These nuclear warheads were so powerful that they made the bombs dropped on Japan resemble firecrackers.

The Balance of Terror

By the end of the 1960s, the United States and the USSR had thousands of such nuclear weapons, more than would be needed to destroy all humankind on earth. Nonetheless, both sides were terrified of falling behind in the arms buildup. As it was, each side was so frightened of the other's weapons that they were afraid to use their own. But each also feared that if the other side gained a big advantage, it would attack.

There had been two world wars already in the twentieth century. Now, according to Richard N. Current, T. Harry Williams, and Frank Freidel:

> [A] wholly new era had arrived, in which another world war could wipe out mankind itself. . . . If humanity was spared an all out war, the reason was perhaps that the world had reached what *The New York Times* . . . called a new balance of terror.[20]

The existence of nuclear weapons—and the possibility that they might be used—cast a terrible shadow over life in the 1960s. The children of the era grew up

Faced with the threat of nuclear war, the nation's schools conducted surprise drills in which students were expected to crouch under their desks for protection against atomic blasts.

with an awareness that they might have no future—that their generation might be wiped out at any moment, along with the rest of life on the planet.

Every U.S. city was studded with little yellow signs that directed people to public buildings and basements that might be used as fallout shelters in case of nuclear attack. Schools conducted drills in which students were instructed in how to fling themselves under their desks and cover their heads against flying debris when the nuclear attack finally came.

Yet, as J. Ronald Oakley, a historian of the age, would write, many feared that "no civil defense system program could be very effective":

> Hiding under desks or tables . . . or burrowing underground in a shelter also seemed to offer little protection against the superbombs . . . even if some did survive the immediate blast or the first few days of fallout, what would be the point of coming out of the shelters to a world of burned forests, flattened cities, contaminated water and food and air, lingering radiation sickness, and anarchy, where the human race would act like animals in the jungle? Television and radio were already carrying stories of people hoarding supplies in their own little bomb shelters and promising to shoot anyone who approached their sanctuary in a postatomic world.[21]

Meanwhile, with both countries carrying out nuclear weapons tests, radioactive material was already being released into the atmosphere. Some contaminated material was even found in cow's milk. Parents and some doctors worried about the future medical effects on their children.

Tensions over Cuba

In 1959 the dictatorial Cuban regime of Fulgencio Batista y Zaldívar was overthrown by a revolution led by a young lawyer named Fidel Castro. Cuba, the small island country about ninety miles off the shore of Florida, was best known to Americans as a good place for a Caribbean-style vacation.

Batista had been a brutal ruler who had all but abolished civil rights in Cuba. Few Americans were sad to see the dictator go, and the U.S. government rushed to recognize the new government in Cuba. It was not long, however, before trouble began to develop between Castro and the United States.

Fidel Castro, communist leader of Cuba. Because of Cuba's proximity to the United States, American officials worried over Russian involvement in and support of Castro's regime.

Many people suspected that Castro was a communist. He denied it, but at the same time he made it clear that his government would not join the Western bloc in opposition to the Soviet Union. This made the American government both nervous and suspicious. What if Castro were a communist, after all? Could the United States tolerate a communist nation—and a Soviet ally—ninety miles off its own shores?

Tensions between the United States and Cuba escalated throughout 1960 and early 1961. Castro repeatedly denounced what he called "Yankee imperialism." In August 1960 he seized all American-owned property in Cuba.

In the United States, anti-Castro Cuban exiles, who had poured into the country after the revolution, demanded that the United States take action against Castro. Meanwhile, Soviet premier Nikita Khrushchev publicly suggested that if the United States dared to take military action against its neighbor, the Soviet Union might "support Cuba with rocket fire." [22]

The U.S. government refused to heed the Russian threat. As far as the United States was concerned, if Fidel Castro was not a communist, he might as well be. By the time John F. Kennedy was sworn in as president, plans were already under way to invade Cuba.

The Bay of Pigs

The invasion of Cuba was to be carried out by some 1,500 to 2,000 Cuban exiles, trained and equipped by the Central Intelligence Agency (CIA). It was a small force, but Castro had begun his own revolution with a smaller force than that. The exiles

Living with Fear

From the late 1950s through the 1960s, Americans lived with the constant fear of Soviet attack. There was the ominous sense that, at any moment, the sirens might sound and atomic bombs might fall from the sky— bombs more terrible than anything humankind had ever experienced. As J. Ronald Oakley described in his book God's Country: America in the Fifties, *"No one really knew . . . how great the destruction would be."*

"Although Americans learned to live with the fear, it was always there: newspapers, television programs, magazines, and government reports provided a steady stream of information about what would happen to America's cities if the bombs fell. . . .

In 1958 and 1959, a special Radiation Subcommittee of the Joint Committee on Atomic Energy did a study of the hypothetical impact of a Russian atomic attack on the United States. The study focused on the possible effects if Russia had dropped a series of hydrogen bombs totalling 1,500 megatons (a moderate, not heavy, bomb attack) on America's cities and military installations. . . . Released in June of 1959, the study contained some very disturbing conclusions. Twenty million Americans would be killed on the first day and 22 million more would die in the following sixty days from radiation sickness, making a grand total of 42 million, 28 percent of the population. The east coast would be destroyed by the explosion of the bombs and resulting fire storms, and the percentage of the population killed here would be especially high—65 percent in metropolitan New York, 91 in Boston, 80 in Philadelphia, 92 in Baltimore, and 81 in the capital. . . . The attack would bring burned forests and cropland, urban rubble, erosion, floods, fires, food shortages, medical service shortages, a panicky and perhaps disorderly population, the breakdown of transportation and communication, and the interruption of almost all governmental, industrial, and medical services. There would also be long-term environmental and climatic changes. . . . For decades to come, there would be diseases and death from radioactive fallout. The country could survive and rebuild, and ecological balance would be gradually restored, but it would take a long time, the report concluded."

and the CIA believed that once the attack started the invaders would be joined by thousands of anti-Castro Cubans.

The new president was informed of the plan and asked to authorize U.S. air support for the invading forces. Kennedy was

Cuba

reluctant to involve the armed forces directly. He allowed the invasion to go ahead, but refused U.S. air support.

The landing took place on a beach at the Bay of Pigs, south of Havana. Much to the shock of the attackers, there was no popular uprising to support them. Trapped in a nearby swamp, a majority of the invading force was captured within two days.

Any chance that the United States and Cuba might settle their differences peacefully had come to an end. An outraged Castro was more firmly entrenched in power than ever. Meanwhile, Khrushchev promised to support Cuba against any further U.S. aggression. Cuba was grateful for the superpower's help. Whether or not Castro had been a communist from the beginning, the Soviet Union now had an ally in America's backyard.

The failed invasion was a blow to the prestige of the new American president, and of America itself. To many observers, America seemed not only foolish but weak. It had acted like a bully and gotten its own nose bloodied.

Kennedy publicly took full responsibility for the fiasco. The president's support-

ers, however, pointed out that the invasion had not been his idea. Meanwhile, the embittered Cuban exiles grumbled that if Kennedy had provided air support, they might have done better.

The Berlin Wall

Shortly after the Bay of Pigs, the United States—and the Western bloc—faced a serious challenge from the communists in Europe. The opposition came from the Soviet-occupied defeated nation of Germany, which the victorious powers had divided after World War II.

East Germany was part of the Eastern bloc, while West Germany was allied with the West. The nation's biggest city, Berlin, was divided as well. Although the entire city was inside East Germany, West Berlin was under the control of the Western powers. The rest of the city, called East Berlin, was in the hands of the Soviets.

West Germany and West Berlin were more prosperous than East Berlin. Many East Germans wanted to live in West Germany; however, the East German government had laws designed to keep them in the East. Despite these laws, thousands of East Germans continued to move to the West. Among them were some of the most skilled and educated people in the country.

The easiest place for East Germans to slip into the West was Berlin. Tens of thousands of East Berliners crossed into the western part of the city each day. They went either to work, to shop, or to visit friends or family members. Many of them never came back. For East Germany, Berlin was like an open wound, draining it of the human power it needed to rebuild from the war. For the Soviet Union, it was a humiliation—a daily reminder that many East Germans preferred life in the capitalist West to communism.

Early in the morning of August 13, 1961, East German soldiers appeared in the streets of Berlin. Weapons at the ready, they set about stringing barbed wire across the city. It was the first step in the construction of the Berlin Wall—a series of physical barriers that would seal off West Berlin from East Germany. The number of places where people could cross back and forth between East and West Berlin was severely limited, and passage across them was tightly controlled. Armed guards were placed along the entire border with West Berlin, ready to shoot anyone attempting to sneak across the wall.

The Cold War Heats Up

The temperature of the Cold War shot up dramatically with the construction of the Berlin Wall. In protest against the Soviets' action, Western nations moved a thousand tanks to the East German border. A few days later, the Soviets resumed testing atomic weapons, a practice that both sides had only recently stopped as a gesture of goodwill. There was very little goodwill left.

The Soviets demanded that the Western powers leave Berlin. They refused. A group of American officials attempting to cross into East Berlin were prevented by border guards. They protested. American tanks were brought to the western side of the border crossing. Soviet tanks moved into place across from them. For a time, it looked as though tank warfare might break out in the streets of Berlin. After sixteen hours, however, the Soviet tanks withdrew. The immediate danger was past, but Berlin remained a flash point in the Cold War.

In June 1963, President Kennedy visited West Berlin to demonstrate the West's continued commitment to the city. Speaking from a podium overlooking the wall, Kennedy declared, "All free men, wherever they may live, are citizens of Berlin,

Europe During the Cold War

Denmark
Netherlands
Britain
Berlin
East Germany
USSR
Poland
Belgium
Luxembourg
West Germany
Czechoslovakia
Switzerland
Austria
Hungary
France
Italy
Romania
Yugoslavia
Spain
Albania

Soviet-Controlled Eastern Europe

and therefore, as a free man, I take pride in the words 'Ich bin ein Berliner [I am a Berliner].'"[23]

The Berlin Wall remained a symbol of the Cold War throughout the 1960s and beyond. Built not to keep invaders out but to keep East Germans in, the wall was a chilling reminder of the divisions between East and West.

The Cuban Missile Crisis

Even while the world's attention was focused on Berlin, tensions were rising again between the United States and Cuba. Embarrassed by the Bay of Pigs, Kennedy had launched a campaign to oust Castro from Cuba.

Publicly banning trade with the small island country, the president secretly approved a covert campaign of sabotage against Cuba. Code-named Operation Mongoose, it included assassination attempts on Castro himself, such as a bizarre attempt to poison his famous cigars.

Meanwhile, pressure was put on Cuba by the staging of elaborate U.S. military exercises in the Caribbean. The armed forces carried out mock invasions of nearby islands, suggesting that they were training for a new attack on Cuba itself.

The American efforts to intimidate Cuba angered Khrushchev. Cuba's economic success was important to the Soviet leader. He planned to make the Cuban revolution, and the communist society it was trying to build, a model for future communist revolutions in Latin America. In order to protect Cuba from possible American attack, Khrushchev suggested putting Soviet nuclear missiles in Cuba.

Fidel Castro and Soviet premier Nikita Khrushchev engineered the placement of Russian nuclear warheads within Cuba.

Even though it would make Cuba a nuclear target of the United States, Castro agreed to accept the weapons.

Defending Cuba was not the only reason for placing missiles on the island. Both Khrushchev and Castro felt that it was important for the balance of power to be maintained. The communist bloc was at that time at a disadvantage when it came to ballistic missiles. The Western military alliance known as NATO had installed U.S. missiles in Turkey, very near the Soviet border. The Soviets had no missiles that close to the United States. Cuba would provide them with the base they needed to restore the balance of terror.

The first of the Soviet missiles were installed in total secrecy. On October 14,

1962, an American U2 spy plane on a routine mission over Cuba took photographs of what turned out to be Soviet missile sites. American analysts quickly recognized them for what they were and reported the news to Kennedy. Once the missiles were fully in place, the president's advisers feared, the Soviets would be able to launch a nuclear attack on major U.S. cities, and the United States would have no time to respond.

For more than a week, Kennedy and his advisers kept the discovery of the missiles secret while they decided what to do. Then, on October 22, Kennedy went on television to address the nation. The United States, the president declared, had "unmistakable evidence" that the Soviets had "offensive" nuclear missiles in Cuba.

[T]his secret, swift and extraordinary build-up of Communist missiles, in an area well known to have a special and historical relationship to the United States . . . is a deliberately provocative and unjustified change in the status quo which cannot be accepted by this country.[24]

One way or another, the president was determined that the missiles had to be removed. As a first step, he announced a naval quarantine of Cuba. All ships attempting to reach the island would be searched for weapons. If weapons were found, the ships would be turned back on the high seas. The possibility of a confrontation between the United States and the Soviet Union was clear. So was the danger that a confrontation could lead to all-out war.

Nuclear Confrontation Less Likely

One effect of the Cuban missile crisis was to inspire the Soviet Union to what some U.S. observers, including foreign policy adviser Henry Kissinger, saw as a drastic buildup of their nuclear forces. In his book Years of Upheaval, *Kissinger described the change in the nuclear balance that took place following the missile crisis.*

"Vietnam War expenditures had tilted the defense budget toward consumables for military operations [in Southeast Asia], leaving many gaps in our force structure. . . . We had lived for over a decade through a revolution in technology. After their humiliation in the Cuban missile crisis of 1962 . . . the Soviets started a relentless building program to catch up with us in strategic [nuclear] forces. This was bound in time to challenge the basis of our strategy since 1945: the reliance on superior American strategic nuclear power. . . . By the beginning of Nixon's second term [in 1973], the Soviets had achieved parity in numbers of [intercontinental missiles] and superiority in [the total power and weight of nuclear warheads]. Thus, resort to strategic nuclear war as the principal instrument of defense became less and less credible."

"We will not prematurely or unnecessarily risk the costs of world-wide nuclear war in which even the fruits of victory would be ashes in our mouth," Kennedy declared. "[B]ut neither will we shrink from that risk at any time it must be faced." [25]

It seemed that the United States was willing to take the world to the brink of nuclear war, and even to push it over, if the Soviets did not remove the missiles.

Direct confrontation was likely to come within days. Several Soviet ships were already on the way to Cuba. By October 24, they would reach the rim of the American quarantine. By that time, U.S., Soviet, and Cuban forces had all been put on full alert. All the while, the Soviet ships drew closer and closer to the seemingly inevitable confrontation. Then, not far from the quarantine line, they began to turn back.

A feeling of tremendous relief swept the world, as news of the turnabout was broadcast. "We were eyeball to eyeball," Secretary of State Dean Rusk told his colleagues. "And the other side just blinked." [26]

The relief, however, was premature. An immediate confrontation had been avoided, but the crisis was not over. Soviet ships had turned back, but they could easily change course again. Besides, there were still ballistic missiles in Cuba. What was to be done about them? However close the world had been to nuclear war, it would soon get even closer.

Khrushchev sent a message to Kennedy:

You and I should not now pull on the ends of the rope in which you have tied the knot of war. The harder you and I pull, the tighter the knot will become. Then the knot will have to be cut. What that would mean, I need not explain to you. [27]

The premier quickly followed up his ominous message with a hopeful offer. The Soviets would pull their missiles out of Cuba, he said, if the United States would take its own missiles out of Turkey—*and* promise not to invade Cuba.

Khrushchev wanted to bring the crisis to an end. He was worried that things were getting out of control. He knew that some of his military officers in Cuba were getting trigger-happy; he suspected there were high-ranking officers in the American military who were looking for an excuse to invade Cuba—and perhaps to set off a confrontation between the superpowers as well. If things were not settled soon, war hawks on either side might take matters into their own hands.

Almost immediately, some of them began to do just that. The United States had continued to send spy planes over Cuba throughout the crisis. Now, with a settlement apparently in the offing, Soviet military officers in Cuba shot down one of the U2 planes, killing the pilot.

Preparing for Invasion

Suddenly the crisis was back at the flash point. Did the shootdown mean that Khrushchev's offer had been a blind? Were the military forces in Cuba beyond Moscow's control? What was really happening?

The Americans seriously considered an immediate invasion of Cuba. Preparations for an invasion had already been made, as well as for an air strike designed to wipe out all the ballistic missiles on the ground. In any case, the missiles did not appear ready to be launched. With any luck, some

Labels on image:
ERECTOR ON LAUNCH PAD
MISSILE READY BLDGS
OXIDIZER VEHICLES
PROB HYDROGEN PEROXIDE TANKS
MISSILE READY BLDGS
FUELING VEHICLES
TENTS
ERECTOR ON LAUNCH PAD
MISSILE ON TRAILER

An aerial photograph indicates the storage facilities and launching positions of nuclear weapons in Cuba.

military leaders thought, a quick, massive strike against Cuba could oust Castro, destroy the missiles, and deal a resounding blow to the prestige of the communist bloc.

What the Americans did not know was that the ballistic missiles were not the only nuclear weapons in Cuba. The Soviets also had several smaller, tactical nuclear weapons on the island. What is more, they had already decided to use them against any invasion attempt. The Americans had no way to know this, but any American attack would almost certainly mean the outbreak of a nuclear exchange. Fortunately for the future of the world, Kennedy decided not to invade. At least not right away. Instead, he told the Soviet ambassador that if the missiles were removed he would publicly pledge not to invade Cuba.

Kennedy hoped that this offer would be enough, but the Soviet ambassador pressed the president. What about the U.S. missiles in Turkey? Kennedy could not publicly promise to remove them, the ambassador was told. The president

would have to consult NATO. The missiles in Turkey were under NATO command. Kennedy did, however, promise privately that they would be removed. That, it turned out, was enough for the Soviets.

The agreement was announced on October 27, 1962. The Soviets would remove their missiles from Cuba, and the United States would promise not to invade Cuba. The crisis was over, and so was the threat of imminent nuclear war. At least for the moment.

In April 1963, the last condition of the deal was faithfully fulfilled: NATO missiles were removed from Turkey.

In some way, the Cuban missile crisis actually seemed to ease tensions between the superpowers. Perhaps it helped them to understand each other better. The Cold War would continue, not only throughout the 1960s, but through the 1970s and 1980s as well. The United States and the Soviet Union never came so close to nuclear confrontation again.

Chapter

4 The Race for the Moon

Ironically, the hard realities of the Cold War would lead to the fulfillment of one of humankind's most romantic fantasies. Human beings had always looked to the heavens with awe and longing. Once it became clear that the lights they saw in the sky were not just lights, but places, people began to dream of going to them.

It was only a dream, however, at least until the Wright brothers managed to rise into the air with a heavier-than-air craft at Kitty Hawk, North Carolina, in 1903. A few decades later, airplanes were traveling hundreds of miles at a time, and even crossing the Atlantic. But even then, space—that vast unknown universe beyond Earth's gravity—seemed unreachable. The air was one thing—space was another.

Science fiction writers fantasized about escaping gravity and visiting other planets in space, but most people had too much common sense to believe that such a thing could really happen. But it was possible for man to leave the earth's atmosphere. In the 1960s, it would actually be done.

The Space Race

Scientists had known for a long time that space travel was more than a dream. Scien-

tifically, it was completely possible. What was a dream, however, was to find the millions of dollars needed to institute the research and development for this massive undertaking.

There was an enormous amount of basic science to explore: theoretical work in fields like gravitation, propulsion, thermodynamics, materials science, and others. And, after all that was done, there would be the tremendous expense of building huge rockets, and super-high-tech, state-of-the-art space vehicles, most of which could only be used once. Only a national government, or combination of governments, had the resources that would be needed for such a project.

Governments, however, were not in the business of turning dreams into reality. They needed hard, practical reasons to devote huge amounts of their national resources to scientific projects. The space sciences seemed a frivolous expense to most American politicians—until World War II opened their eyes to the military potential of space.

That reason was provided by the Cold War. The competition between the United States and the Soviet Union influenced almost every major decision of both governments. When it came to science, the fact that one country was researching and developing was often reason enough for the other one to attempt it too, particularly when the project had military implications. And few fields had more military implications than the space sciences.

The same technology that would allow a nation to send a rocket into space would help send a missile carrying a bomb across an ocean, and vice versa. In 1958, President Eisenhower had signed a bill establishing the National Aeronautics and Space Administration (NASA). NASA's job was to conduct research and development on the exploration and uses of space.

The Soviets Take the Lead

The initial big step into space would be to send a man-made object high enough to go into orbit around the earth. The Soviets got there first. On October 4, 1957, they launched the first *Sputnik Zemli* or "traveling companion of the world." *Sputnik I*—as it was called for short—was a 184-pound capsule packed with scientific instruments that could radio information about conditions in space back to Earth.

Americans were stunned by the Soviet achievement. Some even refused to believe it. They thought the Soviets were lying. But American scientists and U.S. political leaders knew that it was true. The Soviets clearly had more powerful rockets than the United States. To the American leaders, this was intolerable. Ironically, according to authors Hugo Young, Bryan Silcock, and Peter Dunn:

If any single moment can be seen to have made Project Apollo [the U.S. program to put human beings on the moon] inevitable, this was it. The moment Sputnik went aloft can be seen as

the beginning of the transformation of the American space program into an arm of diplomacy, security and psychology at the center of America's international objectives. Instead of proceeding into space with the well-ordered calm of the leader in the field, the United States suddenly discovered that it had lost what appeared to be a race for the elusive and potent goal "prestige" in the eyes of the world. It was a shattering revelation.[28]

Within two months, the Soviets had launched *Sputnik II,* a much larger satellite that carried the first living creature into space, a dog named Laika.

The United States had been planning to send its own satellite into orbit, but the Soviets had beaten them. And beaten them badly. What is more, even *Sputnik I* had been heavier than the planned U.S. satellite would be. *Sputnik II* weighed a whopping 1,100 pounds.

The United States finally launched its own first satellite, *Explorer 1,* on January 1, 1958, from Cape Canaveral, Florida. Eventually, the United States would take the lead in the number of satellites put into orbit around the earth. In most respects, however, the Soviet Union would stay ahead in the race into space well into the 1960s.

In the Cold War world of the late 1950s and early 1960s, that was a chilling thought. Rockets that could carry instruments and people into space could carry weapons there too. Even nuclear weapons.

Aiming at the Moon

Putting objects into orbit was only the first step in leaving the earth. The next step was sending a man-made object to another heavenly body. The closest heavenly body to Earth was the moon.

Both the United States and the Soviet Union attempted to send unmanned probes to the moon as early as 1958. Both efforts failed. The next year, however, the Soviet *Luna* (or *Lunik*) *II* actually crashed into the moon. The capsule, which looked something like a metallic soccer ball, sent back valuable data about the atmosphere around the moon before it hit. The next month *Luna III* sent back the first pictures from the dark, or far, side of the moon—a region that human beings had only been able to imagine before.

Men in Space

On April 12, 1961, a Soviet cosmonaut named Yuri Gagarin became the first human being in space, when he circled the earth in the Soviet orbiter *Vostok 1*. The flight lasted one hour and forty-eight minutes and reached an altitude of 187 miles.

On May 5, 1961, a Redstone rocket lifted off from a launching pad at the U.S. space center at Cape Canaveral for the first manned U.S. space flight. *Mercury 3* carried the *Freedom 7* space capsule and U.S. naval commander Alan B. Shepard Jr., reaching a maximum altitude of 116.5 miles into the sky. The flight only lasted a quarter of an hour before the capsule dropped back to Earth, splashing down in the Atlantic near the Bahamas. In that fifteen minutes, the United States had put an American into space. In one respect, they had even beaten the Soviets. Shepard had managed to steer his craft, if only clumsily, by using small rockets on the sides of the vehicle to alter its course.

Alan B. Shepard Jr., the first U.S. astronaut in space, piloted his own craft during the historic journey.

The following February, Colonel John H. Glenn Jr. became the first American to orbit the earth, as Yuri Gagarin had done. During his five-hour *Mercury 5* flight, Glenn flew around the planet three times before returning to the earth's surface.

A New Ocean

When it came to space travel, the United States was still a fledgling in the Soviets' wake. Richard Nixon, the loser in the presidential race, asked:

[W]hy then are we behind in our space program? I would say the reason we are behind in developing the very large-size rockets which are needed to put large payloads in outer space is that we did little to begin our ballistic missile program until the mid-50s, whereas the Russians began to make an all-out effort in this particular area in 1946 and 1948.[29]

The United States was still behind when Kennedy took office in January 1961. As a candidate, Kennedy had attacked the Republicans for being behind in the space race. Now, as president, he was determined that the United States must take the lead—and do it in a dramatic way.

Spurred on by Vice President Lyndon B. Johnson, the head of the Space Council, Kennedy decided that the United States would go to the moon. Speaking to Congress in May 1961, he declared that the United States would land a man on the

Spaceship Earth

Many reasons have been given for going into space, some by scientists, some by science fiction writers, and some by poets and philosophers. In the Apollo 11 *astronauts' own book,* First on the Moon, *Neil Armstrong suggests a reason that uniquely reflects his background as an astronaut.*

"After all, the earth itself is a spacecraft. It's an odd kind of spacecraft, since it carries its crew on the outside instead of inside. But it's pretty small. And it's cruising in an orbit around the sun. It's cruising in an orbit around the center of a galaxy that's cruising in some unknown orbit, in some unknown direction and at some unspecified velocity. . . . It's hard for us to get far enough away from this scene to see what's happening. If you're in the middle of a crowd, the crowd appears to extend in every direction, as far as the eye can see. You have to step back and look down from the Washington Monument or something like that to see . . . that the whole picture is quite a bit different from the way it looks when you are in the middle of all those people. From our position on the earth, it is difficult to observe where the earth is, and where it's going, or what its future course might be. Hopefully, by getting a little farther away, both in the real sense and the figurative sense, we'll be able to make some people step back and reconsider their mission in the universe, to think of themselves as a group of people who constitute the crew of a spaceship going through the universe. If you're going to run a spaceship you've got to be pretty cautious about how you use your resources, how you use your crew, and how you treat your spacecraft."

surface of the moon, and it would bring him safely back to the earth. What is more, it would do so "before the decade is out."

No single space project in this period will be more impressive to mankind, or more important. . . . In a very real sense, it will not be one man going to the moon . . . it will be an entire nation. For all of us must work to put him there. . . . This is not merely a race. Space is open to us now; and our eagerness to share its meaning is not governed by the efforts of others. We go into space because whatever mankind must undertake, free men must fully share.[30]

It was a daring pledge. It was also an expensive one; the proposed program would cost billions of dollars. No one really knew whether it was possible to go to the moon that quickly. If the United States attempted to accomplish the plan and failed, not just the president but the country would look foolish and boastful. Nonetheless, Congress voted to approve the project, and the national commitment to space surged ahead.

Congress and the majority of the country apparently agreed with the president. "This is the new ocean," Kennedy had said, "and I believe the United States must sail upon it."[31]

Gemini Flights

Before Americans could land on the moon, they would have to learn to fly in space. The first giant step in the American voyage to the moon was the Gemini manned space flight program. It was called Gemini after the constellation of stars named for the twin sons of Zeus, because the Gemini flights were designed for two astronauts.

It was known from the start that a moon landing would require more than one person, as well as more than one space vehicle. One vehicle would be needed to carry both the astronauts and a smaller landing craft from Earth into orbit around the moon. Another vehicle, the lunar ex-

Fearing Soviet dominance in the space race, President Kennedy vowed before Congress in 1961 that the United States would land an astronaut on the moon before the end of the decade.

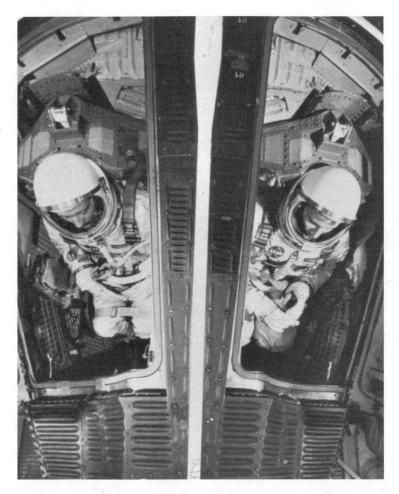

Astronauts are strapped in a space capsule during a Gemini mission. The Gemini program was instrumental in teaching astronauts how to maneuver their crafts, dock with other ships, and even walk in the airless, weightless environment of space.

cursion module, or LEM, would serve as the landing craft which would then carry one or more astronauts to the surface. At least one other astronaut would be needed to stay with the mother ship until the LEM returned with its passengers, and they could all return to Earth.

On March 23, 1965, astronauts Virgil "Gus" Grissom and John W. Young boarded *Gemini 3* to become the first two-man crew to conduct in-orbit maneuvers of a manned spacecraft during flight.

A few months later, *Gemini 4* took off on June 3, 1965, with Air Force Major Edward H. White II and astronaut James Mc-

Divitt aboard. During that flight, White became the first American not only to walk in space—when he slid outside the capsule and floated for thirty-six minutes at the end of a tether—but also to use a personal propulsion pack during a space walk. This floating-tether technique, which the Soviets had already experimented with, would allow space travelers to make adjustments and repairs to the outside of their vehicle in flight.

Before the Gemini program ended in 1966, spacecraft had been developed that could perform tricky maneuvers in space. They could even dock with each other,

In 1963 the Soviet Union put the first female cosmonaut into space. Valentina Tereshkova (pictured here with Yuri Gagarin) orbited the earth for more than seventy hours.

allowing people to move from one craft to another. This would be vital to putting a man on the moon. That was the way the great project was always described: "putting a *man* on the moon." And man was not used to mean "human being of either sex." It meant man. There was no question that the first person on the moon would be male.

The scientists of NASA acted like old-time sailors who claimed that it was bad luck to have a woman aboard ship. They considered space travel an adventure for men only. And, in the 1960s, the American public—including most American women—saw nothing narrow or unfair about that.

The Soviet Union put the first woman cosmonaut, Valentina V. Tereshkova, into orbit for almost seventy-one hours as early as 1963. No American woman would join her in the entire decade. In fact, it would be twenty years after Tereshkova's voyage

before astronaut Sally K. Ride would board the shuttle *Challenger* and become the first American woman in space.

Tragedy on the Launching Pad

Gemini was followed by the Apollo program, which would complete the plans to put a man on the moon. But first, a series of unmanned surveyor flights sent back thousands of pictures of the surface of the moon. These allowed NASA scientists to choose the spot for the eventual touchdown of a manned Apollo spacecraft. That turned out to be a region that was happily named the Bay of Tranquillity.

However, the Apollo program got off to a tragic start. Its first flight was to be a three-man, fourteen-orbit trip around the earth, scheduled to begin on February 21, 1967. Before that could happen, however, there would be painstaking simulations of every step in the process, short of actual liftoff. Nothing would be left to chance.

On January 27, during a routine test, the three astronauts scheduled to make the first flight climbed into their *Apollo 1* capsule atop a powerful Saturn rocket on the launchpad at Cape Kennedy, formerly Cape Canaveral. They strapped themselves into the seats in which they were to soar into space less than a month in the future.

Suddenly, in the midst of the long countdown and check of equipment—the same countdown that would be performed in the moments leading up to the actual flight—the pure oxygen that formed the atmosphere inside the tightly closed capsule burst into flame.

"Get us out of here!"[32] shouted one of the men. But it was too late. All three men died in the flash fire. They were Ed White, the veteran of *Gemini 4;* Gus Grissom, the second American in space; and Roger B. Chaffee, an astronaut preparing for his first space flight.

Only four days later, two more astronauts were killed in a fire in a flight simulator at NASA's facility in Houston, Texas. A temporary halt was ordered to all manned flights. For a time, it seemed that the Apollo program was ended, and that the dream of landing Americans on the moon during the 1960s was doomed along with it.

Riders on the Earth

Manned flights were not resumed until the fall of 1968. Apollo was behind schedule, but there was still time to reach the moon before the end of the decade, if things went well. Kennedy had been dead for five years, but NASA and President Johnson would do their best to keep his promise.

Late in December, *Apollo 8* lifted off from Cape Kennedy, carrying Frank Borman, William A. Anders, and James A. Lovell Jr. Unlike all the manned flights before it, this mission totally burst the chains of the earth's gravity and soared on toward the moon. *Apollo 8* not only reached the moon but continued on around it, making its three passengers the first men to not only orbit the moon but also see its dark side. More importantly, they also saw humanity's own planet from a whole new perspective—a perspective that would impress poets, presidents, and ordinary people alike.

"One Giant Leap for Mankind"

The first human beings arrived on the surface of the moon on July 20, 1969. *Apollo 11*—carrying astronauts Michael Collins, Neil A. Armstrong, and Edwin E. "Buzz" Aldrin Jr.—had left the earth four days earlier on July 16. Now, while Collins stayed with the command vehicle in orbit around the moon, Armstrong and Aldrin manned the LEM for the descent to the moon's surface. The LEM, which had been code-named Eagle, touched down on the Bay of Tranquillity at 4:17 P.M. EDT (Eastern Daylight Time).

"Houston, Tranquillity Base here," Armstrong radioed back to the NASA scientists in Texas. "The Eagle has landed."[33]

The astronauts had had a tense and tiring journey. There was some thought that

"To See the Earth as It Truly Is"

In his first inaugural address—as published in The Inaugural Addresses of the American Presidents—*President Richard M. Nixon spoke not only for the nation but for the world about the effects of man's first sight of Earth from outer space.*

"Only a few short weeks ago we shared the glory of man's first sight of the world as God sees it, as a single sphere reflecting light in the darkness.

As the Apollo astronauts flew over the moon's gray surface on Christmas Eve, they spoke to us of the beauty of earth—and in that voice so clear across the lunar distance, we heard them invoke God's blessing on its goodness. In that moment, their view from the moon moved poet Archibald MacLeish to write:

'To see the earth as it truly is, small and blue and beautiful in that eternal silence where it floats, is to see ourselves as riders on the earth together, brothers on that bright loveliness in the eternal cold—brothers who know now they are truly brothers.'

In that moment of surpassing technological triumph, men turned their thoughts toward home and humanity—seeing in that far perspective that man's destiny on earth is not divisible; telling us that however far we reach into the cosmos, our destiny lies not in the stars but on earth itself, in our own hands, in our own hearts."

A view of Earth from the lunar landscape.

Astronaut Buzz Aldrin stands on the surface of the moon. Millions of people back on Earth watched as Aldrin and astronaut Neil Armstrong conducted their historic moon walk.

they should take time to sleep, so they would be fresh and rested when they ventured out to walk on the moon. But they were too eager to wait.

So at 10:56 P.M. EDT, Neil Armstrong climbed down a ladder from the LEM to become the first human being to set foot on the moon. Incredibly, his walk was beamed back live via television to millions of viewers on Earth.

"That's one small step for man," Armstrong remarked, as he stepped off the ladder, "one giant leap for mankind."

In one sense, that leap was the end of a voyage that had taken all of human history to complete. In another sense, it was only a first step on a much longer voyage, to the planets and beyond.

Although much of the race to the moon had been inspired by the Cold War, there was no hint of nationalism or hostility in the plaque Armstrong and Aldrin left behind when they returned to the earth. It reads: HERE MEN FROM THE PLANET EARTH FIRST SET FOOT UPON THE MOON. JULY 1969 A.D. WE CAME IN PEACE FOR ALL MANKIND.

5 The Civil Rights Movement and the Death of Jim Crow

Even while the U.S. space program was struggling to reach the moon, many Americans were struggling just as hard to obtain their basic human rights here on the earth.

Following the Civil War and emancipation, African Americans had been treated as second-class citizens. In some parts of the country, they were hardly treated as citizens at all. This was especially true in the South, where they were routinely denied the right to vote as well as many other rights taken for granted by white Americans.

Segregation

Whites in the South were determined to continue to dominate the region they had always controlled. When the federal forces finally left the region with the end of Reconstruction in the 1880s, white southerners passed so-called Jim Crow laws. These laws—nicknamed for a popular Negro minstrel song delivered by the performer in blackface—were designed to keep African Americans from competing for jobs and attaining equality in southern society.

Jim Crow was a system of legal segregation—or separation—of blacks and whites, limiting blacks' participation in southern society. For example, African Americans were forbidden to use the same public facilities, to go to the same schools, to stay at the same hotels, to eat at the same restaurants, or even to use the same public washrooms as whites. Marriage between blacks and whites was not only taboo but legally a crime.

For decades, most white Americans accepted segregation as the way things were, even if they did not approve of discrimination. Some believed that separation of the races was God's will. "If God had wanted all men to be one color and to be alike, He would not have made the different races," explained one racist publication. "He knew that races must live apart so they won't

A sign points the way to a separate waiting room for blacks. Such segregation was legal in America through the mid–twentieth century.

mix."[34] Other whites felt that segregation was morally wrong, but believed that it was inevitable in a society in which one group of people had been enslaved for so long.

Even in parts of the country that had no Jim Crow laws, separation of the races was the unwritten rule. One Los Angeles teenager in 1965 complained:

It's not so much that I mind being at an all-Negro school. What I care about is not being able to get together with white kids, or just kids with other backgrounds, and discussing ideas.[35]

Many African Americans bitterly resented segregation, but what could they do? Whites controlled everything: the local governments, the state legislatures and courts, and even the police. For the most part, black southerners simply tried to make the best of life under Jim Crow.

Booker T. Washington, an African American educator and the founder of the Tuskegee Institute in Alabama, argued that African Americans should simply build their own institutions and businesses, and not look to white society for help. W. E. B. Du Bois, the guiding spirit of the National Association for the Advancement of Colored People (NAACP), founded in 1909, felt differently. Washington's beliefs, Du Bois complained,

tended to make the whites, North and South, shift the burden of the Negro problem to the Negro's shoulders. . . . In fact the burden belongs to the nation, and the hands of none of us are clean if we bend not our energies to righting these great wrongs.[36]

Righting those great wrongs was what the civil rights movement of the 1960s set out to do. But that movement—which would destroy Jim Crow—rested on the foundations laid by Du Bois, NAACP activists, and thousands of other brave Americans who had fought racial injustice and bigotry for decades.

Early Victories

The struggle that would finally end legal segregation began in the courts. In 1954 the NAACP won a breakthrough legal victory when the U.S. Supreme Court declared in its famous *Brown v. Board of Education* decision that segregation, or the long-standing policy of separate-but-equal, in the public schools of Topeka, Kansas, was unconstitutional. What's more, it was unconstitutional in public schools everywhere, whether the school facilities were equal or not. "In the field of public education," the Court declared, "separate but equal has no place." Segregated schools were "inherently unequal."

Over the next decade, the Court issued a series of desegregation decisions, outlawing segregation in other public facilities besides schools. African Americans were heartened by these decisions, but court decisions were not enough. Most southern officials simply ignored them.

In December 1955, Rosa Parks, a black woman, refused to move to the back, or black section, of a Montgomery, Alabama, bus when a white person wanted her seat. When she was arrested, the blacks of Montgomery—led by a young minister, Dr. Martin Luther King Jr.—decided to boycott the city's buses until the city recognized their right to sit in any seat they chose.

The Montgomery city government was outraged. A white grand jury charged the

In 1955 Rosa Parks (pictured), a black passenger on an Alabama bus, refused to yield her seat to a white person. Parks's subsequent arrest sparked an African American boycott of the bus system.

Nonviolent Civil Disobedience

Despite the *Brown* decision, more than 98 percent of all school districts that had been segregated in 1954 were still segregated as late as 1963. The reality was that much of the country—and virtually all of the South—still remained segregated long into the new decade. Very few southern restaurants, motels, or other public accommodations were open to both blacks and whites.

The Reverend Dr. Martin Luther King Jr. and other black ministers knew that something more would have to be done if integration was to become a reality. In 1957 they set up an organization known as the Southern Christian Leadership Conference (SCLC) to work toward integration. King suggested that a tactic known as nonviolent civil disobedience be attempted.

Civil disobedience meant openly and deliberately breaking unjust laws, and then willingly enduring the punishment for doing so. This tactic had been recommended by the nineteenth-century American philosopher Henry David Thoreau, who suggested it as a peaceful way to expose the injustice of the laws.

King believed that, by refusing to obey unjust laws and taking their punishment calmly and willingly, blacks would demonstrate the immorality of the laws they defied. Seeing peaceful citizens punished would arouse public sympathy and lead people to change the inequities.

King knew that this nonviolent effort was bound to be met by violence from the other side. Southern whites would not surrender their privileges peacefully. But, no matter what, King preached that the civil rights movement itself would have to remain nonviolent.

boycotters with violating Alabama law, and King and others went to jail. White racists bombed the homes of King and other leaders, but the black residents of Montgomery stubbornly—and proudly—refused to ride the buses. For many blacks of Montgomery, who had put up with segregation all their lives, it felt good to stand up against discrimination at last.

The *Brown* case had changed the legal climate, and the federal courts supported the boycotters. After more than a year, the city was forced to submit and give blacks the same rights on the buses as whites. It was the first great nationally publicized victory against Jim Crow brought about by the united action of ordinary black citizens.

A new kind of civil rights movement had been born in Montgomery. That movement was to change both the face and the heart of America in the 1960s.

Copastor with his father of Ebenezer Baptist Church in Atlanta, King deeply believed in turning the other cheek as the moral response to violence. That was not his only motivation, however, for by refusing to meet violence with violence the protesters would establish their moral superiority to the racists. And, in any event, blacks could never win a violent struggle against the white majority. Nonviolence was not only the movement's best and most moral weapon—it was the only real weapon it had.

The Letter from the Birmingham Jail

The meaning and power of nonviolent civil disobedience was demonstrated by King in Birmingham, Alabama, in 1963. Birmingham's city officials were committed to segregation and bitterly hostile to the civil rights movement. Taking the struggle to the heart of their enemy, the SCLC had targeted Birmingham for what it called Project C—confrontation. The SCLC was determined to desegregate lunchrooms and other public facilities in Birmingham.

When the city authorities denied the SCLC's request for a permit to march in downtown Birmingham, King led a march anyway. This was civil disobedience in action. As expected, he and several other marchers were thrown in jail. From his jail cell that Easter weekend, King wrote a moving letter to some liberal white ministers who had urged him to call off the illegal demonstrations. "You express a great deal of anxiety over our willingness to break laws":

This is certainly a legitimate concern. Since we so diligently urge people to obey the Supreme Court's decision of 1954 outlawing segregation in the public schools, at first glance it may seem

Martin Luther King Jr. (center) became a figurehead of the civil rights movement in the South. King advocated nonviolence, believing that unjust laws could be changed by civil disobedience.

A Long Wait for Justice

Martin Luther King Jr. wrote his famous "Letter from Birmingham Jail" to a group of white ministers. His fellow clergymen had urged him to be more patient and to use less controversial methods. In the following excerpts, published in his book Why We Can't Wait, *King explained as well as anyone ever has why the African Americans' patience had run out.*

"We have waited more than 340 years for our constitutional and God-given rights. The nations of Asia and Africa are moving with jetlike speed toward gaining political independence, but we still creep at horse-and-buggy pace toward gaining a cup of coffee at a lunch counter. Perhaps it is easy for those who have never felt the stinging darts of segregation to say, 'Wait.' But when you have seen vicious mobs lynch your mothers and fathers at will and drown your sisters and brothers at whim; when you have seen hate-filled policemen curse, kick and even kill your black brothers and sisters; when you have seen the vast majority of your twenty million brothers smothering in an airtight cage of poverty in the midst of an affluent society; when you suddenly find your tongue twisted and your speech stammering as you seek to explain to your six-year-old daughter why she can't go to the public amusement park that has just been advertised on television, and see tears welling up in her eyes when she is told that Funtown is closed to colored children, and see ominous clouds of inferiority beginning to form in her little mental sky, and see her beginning to distort her personality by developing an unconscious bitterness toward white people; . . . when you are humiliated day in and day out by nagging signs reading 'white' and 'colored'; when your first name becomes 'nigger,' your middle name becomes 'boy' (however old you are) and your last name becomes 'John,' and your wife and mother are never given the respected title 'Mrs.'; . . . when you are forever fighting a degenerating sense of 'nobodiness'—then you will understand why we find it difficult to wait. There comes a time when the cup of endurance runs over, and men are no longer willing to be plunged into the abyss of despair. I hope, sirs, you can understand our legitimate and unavoidable impatience."

rather paradoxical for us consciously to break laws. One may well ask: "How can you advocate breaking some laws and obeying others?" The answer lies in the fact that there are two types of laws: just and unjust. . . . One has not only a legal but a moral responsibility to obey just laws. Conversely, one has a moral responsibility to disobey unjust laws. I would agree with St. Augustine that "An unjust law is no law at all."[37]

The protesters were determined to show the nation the cruelty of the defenders of Jim Crow laws. While most of the demonstrators acted with calm and dignity, the city police, led by their chief, Eugene "Bull" Connor, behaved like bullying lawbreakers, attacking defenseless demonstrators with clubs, fire hoses, and even attack dogs. They even looked the other way when white racists launched vicious assaults of their own on Birmingham blacks. In one horrible incident, four little girls were killed when racists set off a bomb in a black church during a Sunday service.

Governor Wallace in the Schoolhouse Door

The climax of Project C came when the schools were set to open after summer vacation. Alabama had been ordered to desegregate its schools, but local and state officials balked. Governor George C. Wallace had declared that he would stand in the doors of the schoolhouses rather than let black children enter them.

By then, however, the Birmingham protests had ignited national sympathy for integration. President Kennedy himself called the Alabama National Guard into federal service and ordered it to protect black students enrolling in Alabama schools. Wallace kept his word, symbolically at least, by standing in the doorway of the University of

Governor George Wallace stands before the door of the University of Alabama, barring the admittance of two African American students to the school.

Alabama. But he quickly moved out of the way when National Guard troops ordered him to let two black students enter.

The Children's Crusade

At one point during the Birmingham protests, the SCLC deliberately recruited students from the local elementary and high schools to join in its marches. They called the effort the Children's Crusade. It made sense for young people to be prominent in the civil rights demonstrations. The battle to kill Jim Crow was a battle for their future. In a way, the whole civil rights movement was a Children's Crusade. From the beginning, young people had responded most enthusiastically to the call for protest and civil disobedience.

SNCC

As early as 1960, four black college students had defied an unwritten law that specified "Whites only." They walked up to a segregated lunch counter in a Woolworth store in Greensboro, North Carolina, and sat down. When the black students were ordered to leave, they refused.

Over the next few days, they were joined by other brave young black (and a few white) students. Soon there was no room for ordinary white customers to sit at the counter. No food could be served to anyone, unless it was served to the protesters first. The lunch counter closed.

Other young people launched similar "sit-ins" at other lunch counters around Greensboro. Customers and staff members alike jeered at, heckled, teased, and threatened the protesters. But still they refused to move. Before long, sit-ins were taking place in cities all over the middle South. Local authorities didn't know what to do.

Only two months after the first sit-in, a group of angry young African Americans, who were called together by Ella Baker of the SCLC, met at Shaw University in Raleigh, North Carolina. They founded their own organization, which they dubbed the Student Nonviolent Coordinating Committee (SNCC). The young men and

Black students sit at a "whites only" lunch counter, refusing to leave until they are served. Nonviolent protests like this one rallied support for civil rights organizations across the country and showed how average people could take a stand for freedom.

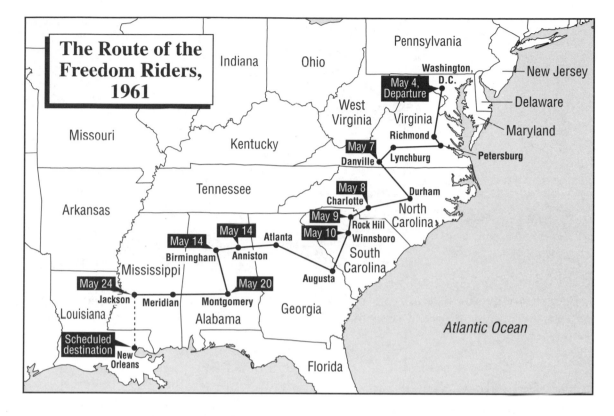

The Route of the Freedom Riders, 1961

womcn of SNCC (pronounced "Snick") were more impatient than the older leaders. The sit-ins had encouraged them to advocate immediate change. The old-line civil rights groups all wanted equality and freedom. SNCC's young militants wanted equality and freedom *now!*

The Freedom Rides

In the spring of 1961, a group of blacks and whites boarded two buses in Washington, D.C., and set off for a historic trip through the Deep South to New Orleans. The Freedom Riders, as they called themselves, were members of the Congress of Racial Equality (CORE). They intended to integrate the bus terminals along their route. "We propose to challenge . . . every form of segregation met by the bus passenger,"[38] a CORE official declared.

It seemed like a simple thing for people traveling together to use the same public rest rooms and eat at the same public restaurants. And yet, the forces of racial bigotry massed to stop them. On May 14, 1961, a mob of Ku Klux Klansmen attacked the Freedom Riders at Anniston, Alabama. One of the buses was firebombed, whilc Klansmen boarded the other and mercilessly beat the people inside. The local police deliberately stayed away until the attack was over.

Undiscouraged, riders continued on their way in the one bus still functioning. They were attacked again at Birmingham. Although they wanted to go on, they could find no bus driver willing to face the

During the Freedom Summer, activists traveled throughout the South registering blacks to vote.

danger of driving them. The first Freedom Rides were ended; however, more would follow.

Freedom Summer

The NAACP, SCLC, SNCC, and CORE each had different philosophies and approaches. In 1964, however, they joined forces to launch Freedom Summer—an all-out black-voter registration drive in Mississippi.

No civil right was more important to southern blacks than the right to vote. In the American political system, votes mean power. But no one can vote without first being registered by local officials. For more than sixty years, whites in the South had kept blacks from registering with a variety of laws that allowed white authorities to declare individual blacks unqualified to vote. Blacks in the South were so often denied the right to vote that most had given up any attempt to register. And no state's officials were more determined to keep blacks from voting than Mississippi's.

Hundreds of young people flooded into Mississippi that summer in an effort to change all that. They set up at least fifty "freedom schools," to teach poor black children about their heritage and their rights. However, they were less successful in convincing black adults to brave the anger and revenge of their white neighbors by registering to vote.

The Violent Response

It was hardly surprising that many African Americans were reluctant to register to vote. No black person who stood up for his or her rights was safe in Mississippi. The NAACP's field secretary for Mississippi, a young black man named Medgar Evers, had been gunned down in his own driveway in June 1963.

Three of the young civil rights workers who came to take part in Freedom Summer mysteriously disappeared soon after they arrived in Mississippi. Michael Schwerner and Andrew Goodwin were white, and James Chaney was black. They had been traveling together in a station wagon in the countryside, investigating one of many burnings of black churches by white racists. Six months later, their bodies were found buried near the small town of Philadelphia, Mississippi. They had been murdered by a group of whites, including some racist policemen.

More than one thousand cases of racist violence were documented in the South between 1956 and 1966. Many more went unrecorded. There were hundreds of bombings and church burnings, beatings, and brutal killings. Lieutenant Colonel Lemuel Penn, a black military officer, was murdered just driving through Georgia on his way to Washington, D.C. Viola Liuzzo, a white woman from Detroit, was shot to death in rural Alabama in 1965 for giving a ride to a young black man after a civil rights demonstration. Vernon Dahmer, who like Medgar Evers worked for the NAACP in Mississippi, was killed in a fire-bombing in Hattiesburg the following year.

The KKK

The worst of the violence came from members of the Ku Klux Klan, or KKK, and other secret organizations, including the local White Citizens Councils that virtually ran many communities. There were actually several Klans who competed with each other for the loyalty and membership fees of white southerners.

The White Knights of the Ku Klux Klan of Mississippi welcomed the civil rights workers with ominous threats in *The Klan Ledger:*

> There is no racial problem here in this state. Our system of strict segregation permits the two races to live in close proximity and harmony with each other and eliminates any racial problem. . . . We are not going to sit back and permit our rights and the rights of our posterity to be negotiated away by . . . atheistic priests, brainwashed black savages, and mongrelized money-worshippers

The Ku Klux Klan attracted white southerners who were opposed to racial integration. The organization was linked to the murder of several individuals, both white and black, who tried to end segregation in the South.

meeting with some stupid or cowardly politician. Take heed, atheists and mongrels, we will not travel your path to Leninist Hell, but we will buy YOU a ticket to the Eternal if you insist. Take your choice, SEGREGATION, TRANQUILITY AND JUSTICE, OR BI-RACISM, CHAOS AND DEATH.[39]

At the height of Klan power in the mid-1960s, total membership was estimated at more than fifty thousand. The killers of Viola Liuzzo and Schwerner, Chaney, and Goodwin were allied with the Klan. Byron de la Beckwith, who killed Medgar Evers, apparently belonged to both the Klan and the White Citizens Council.

Klansmen liked to think of themselves as brave and noble defenders of the southern way of life, but the real bravery and nobility was on the other side—among the young people who faced the dangers and carried on the struggle. In doing so, they gained strength from their belief in the cause of racial justice, from their faith that it would ultimately succeed, and from the solidarity they felt when they joined together to sing. According to Sally Belfrage in her book *Freedom Summer:*

> [W]e stood, everyone, crossed arms, clasped hands and sang "We Shall Overcome." Ending every meeting of more than a half dozen with it, we sang out all fatigue and fear, each connected by this bond of hands to each other. . . . Together we were an army.[40]

Violence Is Tolerated

Although the violence was usually carried out by uneducated bullies, much of it was tolerated, and even tacitly encouraged by what was called the "white power structure" in the South. The power structure included the police who often looked the other way—and sometimes participated in the violence—and southern politicians who spoke against violence in public but encouraged it in private. At one of De la Beckwith's trials for the murder of Medgar Evers, an ex-governor of Mississippi walked into the courtroom and clapped the defendant on the back to signal his support for the man most people assumed was Medgar Evers's killer.

The March on Washington

The forces defending Jim Crow were vicious and deadly, but they were fighting a losing battle. They could carry out a reign of terror in the South. They could frighten individuals and kill many of those who refused to be intimidated. But, in doing so, they lost the support of the American people—including millions of white southerners.

In August 1963, 250,000 Americans traveled to Washington, D.C., to participate in a massive demonstration on behalf of civil rights. It was the largest such demonstration ever held in the nation's capital.

"I still have a dream," Martin Luther King proclaimed to the thousands assembled in front of the Washington Monument. "I have a dream that one day this nation will rise up and live out the true meaning of its creed—we hold these truths to be self-evident, that all men are created equal."[41]

King was speaking not just to the mighty crowd in Washington, but to millions of Americans watching on television.

Martin Luther King Jr. addresses the immense crowd that swarmed the capital during the March on Washington. King's words were carried into the homes of millions of Americans who viewed the event on television.

They were the same Americans who had been watching the Birmingham police attack the Children's Crusade. To most of those millions, the choice between King and Bull Connor was clear.

Black Poverty

Although much of the violence surrounding the civil rights movement occurred in the South, the rest of the nation was not without racial problems. One of the most bitter symptoms of the country's racial divisions was black urban poverty. Some of the worst living conditions in America were in the urban ghettos of northern and west-ern cities where African Americans were packed into crumbling tenements in high-crime neighborhoods that offered few urban services and even fewer jobs.

Young African Americans in these neighborhoods lived under such tension that many were ready to explode. Every now and then a spark would flare, and hundreds of people would take to the streets, fighting, looting, and destroying property. The riots were fueled by rage against the racism the people saw all around them as well as the deteriorating conditions in which they lived. The flare-ups usually occurred in the summertime, when the heat made being indoors unbearable, and restless and angry young men poured into the streets.

The Watts Riot

Riots broke out in several eastern cities in the summer of 1964. In August 1965, word spread through the huge black neighborhood of Los Angeles known as Watts that a black man had been brutally assaulted by the Los Angeles police. The news provoked a fit of rioting and arson that went on for six days, resulting in thirty-four deaths and more than $35 million in property damage.

Police who moved into the neighborhood to quell the riot and firefighters who came to put out the fires were attacked by snipers. Eventually thousands of National

Police officers walk past a victim of the 1965 Watts riot.

Guard troops had to be called to restore order, but not before many square blocks of Watts had been reduced to rubble.

There was no simple, or even rational, reason for the spree of violence with which a minority of the black residents of Watts had destroyed their own homes and businesses. But the riot in Los Angeles brought home to many shocked Americans the real depth of rage and despair that seethed beneath the surface of life in the black ghettos of urban America. While many Americans of all colors were appalled at the self-destructive violence, the riot also produced new calls to end racial discrimination and to correct the economic imbalances that so clearly existed in American society.

Watts was not the end, however. The so-called "long hot summer" of 1967 would see a total of 164 riots break out in many cities, including New York, Toledo, Newark, and Grand Rapids, Michigan, among others. Over one hundred deaths and two thousand injuries occurred in the first nine months of 1967.

Black Power

A growing number of young black militants began challenging traditional civil rights groups like the NAACP and the SCLC. The new militants appealed to the pride of African Americans with slogans like Black Power and Black Is Beautiful. These militants were suspicious of the ideal of integration, which was at the heart of the mainstream civil rights movement.

Stokely Carmichael of SNCC was an early convert to the new Black Power movement. "If you believe in integration," he told liberal whites, "you can come live in Watts. You can send your children to the ghetto schools."[42]

Some Black Power advocates insisted that African Americans should keep themselves apart from whites deliberately and work entirely within their own communities. Some black separatists even called on African Americans to demand land for a black homeland—their own country—as reparation from the U.S. government for slavery.

Most of the young militants verbally attacked the older civil rights leaders as old-fashioned and ineffectual. They rejected as well the commitment to nonviolence; they argued that African Americans should be prepared to defend themselves.

Among the groups that emphasized both black pride and self-defense was the Nation of Islam, or the Black Muslims, headed by the Honorable Elijah Muhammad. Basically a black separatist group, which combined a belief that black people should form their own society with aspects of the Islamic religion, the Nation of Islam gained most of its following in New York and other northeastern cities.

The most prominent Muslim leader next to Muhammad himself was Malcolm X. Malcolm was extremely popular among young black men, who responded to his anger against white America as well as his message of black pride and self-reliance. His influence reached from the streets of Harlem, where his temple was located, to the back roads of the Deep South, where some young SNCC organizers revered him instead of Martin Luther King. Malcolm broke with Elijah Muhammad in 1964; he was gunned down, apparently by Black Muslim assassins, at a New York rally in February 1965.

Another important Black Power group was the Black Panther Party. Party members carried guns; they declared that they were ready to defend themselves against any attack from the police. Several Black Panthers did get involved in gun battles with police. The most prominent was Huey Newton, who was charged with murder in the death of a white Oakland, California, policeman. In 1968, Newton was convicted of involuntary manslaughter and sent to prison.

The Civil Rights Act

Before his death, Kennedy had ordered Democrats in Congress to put together a sweeping civil rights bill. There was some doubt that an effective bill could pass the Congress, however, because powerful white southerners in both houses were experts at blocking legislation.

For a time, Kennedy's assassination cast even more doubt on the bill's future. The new president, Lyndon B. Johnson, was a Texas southerner. He had run for the Democratic presidential nomination himself in 1960, and many prosegregation southerners had supported him. They now hoped that he would kill the civil rights bill. Johnson, the southerner—whom many people had mistaken for a closet segregationist—surprised many people by not only supporting the bill, but pushing hard for its passage.

Thanks to his efforts—and to the wave of affection for Kennedy that followed his death—the Civil Rights Act of 1964 was passed by the Congress, banning all discrimination in public facilities; forbidding racial discrimination in employment, public accommodations, union membership, and all

Malcolm X Speaks to Young People About Nonviolence

On New Year's Day 1965, Malcolm X met with a group of young civil rights fighters from Mississippi at the Hotel Theresa in Harlem. The speech he gave that day was later printed in Malcolm X Talks to Young People. *Many members of his audience who belonged to SNCC believed in nonviolence. Malcolm, however, was skeptical of this philosophy. Less than two months after this talk, Malcolm X was gunned down by black assassins affiliated with the Nation of Islam.*

"So my experience has been that in many instances where you find Negroes always talking about being nonviolent, they're not nonviolent with each other, and they're not loving with each other, and they're not patient with each other, or forgiving with each other. Usually, when they say they're nonviolent, they mean they're nonviolent with somebody else. . . . They are nonviolent with the enemy. . . .

So I myself would go for nonviolence if it was consistent, if it was intelligent, if everybody was going to be nonviolent, and if we were going to be nonviolent all the time. . . . But I don't go along—I'm just telling you how I think—I don't go along with any kind of nonviolence unless everybody's going to be nonviolent. . . .

Now I'm not criticizing those here who are nonviolent. I think everybody should do it the way they feel is best, and I congratulate anybody who can be nonviolent in the face of all that kind of action that I read about in [Mississippi]. But I don't think that in 1965 you will find the upcoming generation of our people . . . who will go along with any kind of nonviolence unless nonviolence is going to be practiced all the way around."

Activist Malcolm X believed that nonviolent civil disobedience was ineffective in producing real changes for black Americans.

federally funded programs; and creating the Equal Opportunity Commission, which guaranteed equal voting rights to blacks.

The Voting Rights Act

But Johnson knew that a white Congress passing laws to protect blacks was not enough. In order to assure blacks their basic democratic rights, Johnson sponsored a powerful voting rights bill in 1965. This bill was so important to Johnson that the president introduced it before an unusual joint session of Congress. "I speak tonight for the dignity of man and the destiny of democracy," the president declared to an all-white Congress:

> At times, history and fate meet at a single time in a single place to shape a turning point in man's unending search for freedom. . . . There is no constitutional issue here. The command of the Constitution is plain. There is no moral issue. It is wrong . . . to deny any of your fellow Americans the right to vote. . . . The effort of American Negroes to secure for themselves the full blessings of American life . . . must be our cause too. Because it is not just Negroes, but really it is all of us who must overcome the crippling legacy of bigotry and injustice.

Then Johnson raised his arms in front of Congress and the nation, and repeated the words of the song sung by the southern blacks and the civil rights workers: "AND—WE—SHALL—OVERCOME!"[43]

Many people in the gallery, and watching on television across America, broke into tears. In his white Texas drawl, the first southern president in nearly half a century had taken on the blacks' and the nation's cause as his own. In their hearts, the racist congressmen and senators who had listened to the president that night already knew that their battle to preserve segregation had been lost.

The Voting Rights Act passed, and Congress passed the Civil Rights Act of 1968, prohibiting housing discrimination and harassment of civil rights workers. By then, African Americans were already making their presence felt as a political force in the South. Even after losing a congressional primary runoff in Mississippi, Medgar Evers's brother Charles was undeterred. "Win, lose, or draw [in this election], we've already won," Evers proclaimed. "They're scared to death. They're going to pay attention to us from now on."[44]

6 The Dream of the Great Society

President Lyndon B. Johnson took the presidential oath of office on the plane back to Washington, D.C., from Dallas on the day of President Kennedy's assassination. The first few months of his presidency were devoted to the unexpected transition from one administration to another.

The Warren Commission

One of the president's most urgent duties was to appoint a commission to investigate Kennedy's assassination. The apparent killer, Lee Harvey Oswald, had been quickly captured, only to be murdered by Jack Ruby as he was being led through the basement of the Dallas jail.

All sorts of questions begged to be answered. Why had Kennedy been assassinated? Had Oswald acted on his own? Or had he been part of some elaborate conspiracy? Wild rumors abounded. Some people suggested that Johnson had been involved, in order to move up to the presidency. Others believed that racist southerners had hired Oswald, because they hoped that, as president, Johnson would kill Kennedy's civil rights legislation. Some claimed that Cuba was involved—or even the U.S. Central Intelligence Agency.

President Johnson gave Earl Warren, chief justice of the Supreme Court, the job of leading the investigation into the assassination. The Warren Commission issued its report in September 1964. It criticized the Secret Service and the FBI for their failure to protect President Kennedy. On the point that most troubled Americans, it concluded that there had been no conspiracy to kill Kennedy. Oswald was a disturbed man, who had been active in the pro-Castro Fair Play for Cuba Committee. He had acted alone.

The Great Society

While the Warren Commission investigated Kennedy's assassination, President Johnson devoted himself to pushing what was left of Kennedy's programs through Congress. Johnson, however, had his own ideas of what the country needed, particularly when it came to social programs. Johnson had been raised in a poor area of Texas, and he had an enormous sympathy for poor people. He also had a strong belief in the need for the federal government to help them.

Speaking to the graduating class of the University of Michigan in 1964, Johnson laid out his hopes for the rest of the century.

"[I]n your time," he told the graduates, "we have the opportunity to move not only toward the rich society and the powerful society, but upward to the Great Society."[45]

Johnson dismissed those he called the "timid souls who say this battle cannot be won, that we are condemned to a soulless wealth." He appealed to the students to join him in the effort to build that Great Society. By that, he meant a society in which all Americans would share significantly in the great wealth and prosperity of the country. Johnson declared:

So let us from this moment begin our work, so that in the future men will look back and say: It was then, after a long and weary way, that man turned the exploits of his genius to the full enrichment of his life.[46]

The War on Poverty

In his 1964 State of the Union address, President Johnson outlined the most important step in his effort to build the Great Society:

This administration today, here and now, declares unconditional war on poverty in America. I urge this Congress and all Americans to join with me

Upon news of Kennedy's death, Vice President Lyndon Johnson (pictured here with Jackie Kennedy) took the oath of office aboard Air Force One.

in that effort. It will not be a short or easy struggle—no single weapon or strategy will suffice—but we shall not rest until that war is won.[47]

To fight this war on poverty, Johnson established some eighty-eight new federal programs and agencies. Among them was a new cabinet-level Department of Housing and Urban Development, as well as a major new federal agency, the Office of Economic Opportunity (OEO).

The OEO was more than a handout agency. It was designed to help the poor help themselves. Even while federal food and welfare programs were being expanded, the OEO was given the job of providing job training and education to poor people and encouraging them to stand up for their own rights.

Johnson's Goals

Jack Valenti was a White House special assistant under Johnson. According to his account, as published in John Sharnik's Inside the Cold War: An Oral History, *the Great Society—which Valenti described as "the most revolutionary upheaval in social legislation that this country's ever seen"—was already born on the day John F. Kennedy died.*

"I was in the motorcade in Dallas when Kennedy was murdered; I was hired by Johnson that very hour. . . . And that night, November 22 [1963], Bill Moyers and myself and the late Cliff Carter spent the night with Lyndon Johnson on the very first night of his Presidency.

I remember we were in his bedroom. He was sprawled out on a vast bed. He had his pajamas on. And that night Johnson painted on a canvas the 'Great Society,' though that night we didn't know it had a name.

He talked at length about how he was going to make it possible for every boy and girl in America to get 'all the education they could take'—by loan, scholarship, or grant. Well, that's the Elementary and Secondary Education Act.

He said . . . 'We're going to have that civil rights bill that's been languishing in the Senate. We're going to get it with no quarter given, and no quarter asked.'

And then he said, 'We're going to do something that Harry Truman tried to do and every President's tried to do: we're gonna get Medicare. We're going to have medical care for the old and the sick in this country who can't afford it.'

And to my bewilderment and puzzlement and surprise, he made it all come true. I might add as an aside—ironic: he never mentioned Vietnam."

Community Action

One of the OEO's most innovative programs was a domestic Peace Corps called Volunteers in Service to America (VISTA). VISTA enlisted idealistic Americans to use their individual knowledge and skills to help poor people and communities implement a variety of local projects designed to improve their lives. They served for two years.

With verve, enthusiasm, and energy, the volunteers helped to organize the poor and previously disenfranchised to become politically active. The volunteers set up Community Action Programs (CAPs) that taught ordinary people how to work together to exert political pressure on local authorities to provide them with services, to protect their neighborhoods, and to repair their public facilities.

Not surprisingly, these community programs were resented by many local governments. Local politicians were accustomed only to business interests demanding action and government resources, not to poor people demanding them as well.

The officials, who accepted OEO money for local projects, had not counted on a bunch of VISTA kids stirring up trouble in their communities. The idea of "stirring up trouble," however, appealed to the VISTA volunteers, just as it did to other young people in the 1960s, and even to President Johnson. As one Johnson aide explained:

> If you send a group of college students or recent college graduates into a situation like that in the VISTA program, you can send them in to teach and to show people how to keep budgets and how to keep house and how to be sani-

tary and how to have hygienic conditions and so forth. But inevitably the VISTA people are going to see that in order to do something, people are going to have to vote, and they're going to have to get control of the city council or the sheriff's office or get on the local board of education . . . Johnson knew that. In my judgment that is what he wanted to happen.[48]

Eventually, however, the local politicians won out. They put pressure on their own parties' representatives in Washington, and before long the VISTA volunteers were ordered to cool their enthusiasm for community action. In the meantime, however, some poor people at least had been empowered; they had gained their first taste of real political involvement.

Medicare and Medicaid

The most important programs of the war on poverty were those that provided medical care to people in need. President Harry S. Truman had asked for a program of national health insurance to cover all Americans as far back as the 1940s. That idea had been rejected at the time. But now, Johnson managed to forge a national consensus, or agreement, that at least the neediest of Americans should have such insurance.

The result was two programs known as Medicare and Medicaid. The Medicare bill, which became law in 1965, was an extension of Social Security that provided medical insurance to the elderly. Medicaid was a joint federal and state program to provide care to poor people of any age.

The Other America

Early in the decade, a sociologist named Michael Harrington published a landmark book entitled The Other America. *In it, he described a problem that had always existed in the United States, but which had long been ignored—the problem of poverty. His book is said to have caught the attention of President Kennedy and helped to inspire the social programs that would eventually be enacted as part of Johnson's war on poverty.*

"There is a familiar America. It is celebrated in speeches and advertised on television and in the magazines. It has the highest mass standard of living the world has ever known.

In the 1950s, this America worried about itself, yet even its anxieties were products of abundance.

. . . The familiar America began to call itself 'the affluent society.' . . . In all this there was an implicit assumption that the basic grinding economic problems had been solved in the United States. In this theory the nation's problems were no longer a matter of basic human needs, of food, shelter, and clothing. Now they were seen as qualitative, a question of learning to live decently amid luxury.

While this discussion was carried on, there existed another America. In it dwelt somewhere between 40,000,000 and 50,000,000 citizens of this land. They were poor. They still are."

Before Medicare, a higher proportion of the elderly were poor because of the expense of medical care. Because of the aging process, seniors need more medical care. Doctors, prescription drugs, and hospital stays were so expensive that the savings of many seniors were quickly eaten up with medical bills. Medicare helped to provide older Americans with proper medical care, while also helping them to retain their savings.

With Truman at his side, Johnson signed the Medicare bill in the Truman Library in Independence, Missouri, Truman's birthplace.

The War in Vietnam

The Great Society was expensive. The war on poverty cost $3 billion in its first three years. It would need even more money in the future, if it were really going to wipe out poverty in America. Johnson believed it was possible. "This great, rich, restless country can offer opportunity and education and hope to all,"[49] he said. But, in saying this, he was not taking the Vietnam War into account.

President Johnson would have liked to devote all his energies—and the bulk of the nation's resources—to building the Great Society. But he could not do so. Unfortunately for his dreams, he had another expensive problem to deal with: a small war he had inherited in the divided country of Vietnam, halfway across the world in Southeast Asia.

Vietnam had once been part of the French colony of Indochina. After the French were driven out in 1956, an election had been scheduled to choose a government for an independent Vietnam. When it became clear that a communist named Ho Chi Minh was virtually certain to win, the election was canceled and the country was divided in two. Ho Chi Minh took over what became North Vietnam, while a government friendly to the West took power in South Vietnam.

By the 1960s, the government of South Vietnam found itself facing a leftist revolution by the National Liberation Front, or Vietcong. The revolutionaries were being supported by North Vietnam.

Not many Americans understood the long and complicated history of Vietnam. Those who did were deeply divided over whether the United States should get involved. Some felt that Vietnam should be left alone to settle its own problems. They saw what was going on there as not much different from the American Revolution in 1775.

But others—including the policy makers of the Johnson administration—saw Vietnam in terms of the Cold War. They believed in what was called "the domino theory." If South Vietnam fell to the communists, they argued, the other small countries of Southeast Asia would fall as well, one by one like a row of dominoes. For these people, the Vietnam War was a contest between freedom and communism.

The United States had first become involved under President Eisenhower, who sent arms and military advisers to Vietnam. Under Kennedy the number of advisers had risen to more than sixteen thousand.

President Johnson signs the Medicare bill, a measure that guaranteed medical insurance for the poor.

They were supposedly there only to help train and advise the South Vietnamese military. More and more, however, the advisers were becoming involved in directing and fighting the war themselves.

In 1964, the first full year of Johnson's presidency, 136 Americans were killed in Vietnam. That was almost twice as many as in 1963, which was, in turn, almost twice as many as the year before.

The Tonkin Gulf Resolution

In the presidential election of 1964, the Republican candidate, Barry S. Goldwater, attacked Johnson for fighting a limited war in Vietnam. If the United States was going

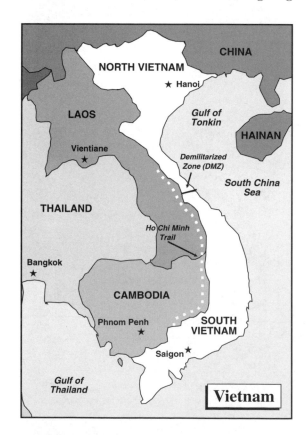

Vietnam

to fight a war, Goldwater insisted, it should go all out—even to the point of bombing Vietnam "into the stone age."

Johnson quoted Thomas Jefferson to justify his policy of limited war in Vietnam. "It is the melancholy law of human societies to be compelled sometimes to choose a great evil in order to ward off a greater." [50] By fighting a small war, Johnson hoped to avoid having to fight a major war.

Johnson was widely regarded as the dove, or peace candidate, in 1964. Goldwater—who had hinted at using nuclear weapons in Vietnam—was considered the war hawk.

Even so, Johnson had already won from Congress the right to escalate, or intensify, American involvement in the war before the election took place. In August 1964, the U.S. Navy reported that its destroyer *Maddox* had been attacked by North Vietnamese gunboats in the Gulf of Tonkin, off the shore of North Vietnam. In return, the United States had launched attacks against several North Vietnamese military boats in the area, destroying many of them.

The attack on the *Maddox* was considered an act of war. Johnson used the occasion to obtain from Congress permission "as the President determines, to take all necessary steps, including the use of armed force" [51] to defend U.S. forces in Southeast Asia. The so-called Tonkin Gulf Resolution passed the House of Representatives unanimously and the Senate by a vote of eighty-eight to two. One of the two senators who voted against it was Wayne Morse, who denounced it as a "pre-dated declaration of war." [52]

The United States never did actually declare war in Vietnam. This caused many Americans to denounce the war as unconstitutional. Even without a declaration of

The Gulf of Tonkin Resolution

In addition to giving a reason for America's military activities in Southeast Asia, the Gulf of Tonkin Resolution served in place of a formal declaration of war. The following excerpts are taken from Leon Friedman and Burt Neuborne's Unquestioning Obedience to the President.

"Congress approves and supports the determination of the President, as Commander-in-Chief, to take all necessary measures to repel any armed attack against the forces of the United States and to prevent further aggression. . . .

The United States regards as vital to its national interest and to world peace the maintenance of international peace and security in Southeast Asia. Consonant with the Constitution and the Charter of the United Nations and in accordance with its obligations under the Southeast Asia Collective Defense Treaty [which South Vietnam had signed], the United States is, therefore, prepared, as the President determines, to take all necessary steps, including the use of armed force, to assist any member or protocol state of the Southeast Asia Collective Defense Treaty requesting assistance in defense of its freedom."

war, however, President Johnson and his successor, Richard M. Nixon, would use the Tonkin Gulf Resolution—and the vested power of the presidency—to wage war in Southeast Asia for nearly ten more years.

Troop Escalation

By the end of 1965, there were 150,000 American troops in Vietnam. By the end of 1966, there would be 389,000. At one point in 1966, more Americans were being killed in the fighting than Vietnamese. In 1963, less than 100 Americans had been killed in Vietnam. By 1967, it was no longer unusual for 100 Americans to die in a single week.

As the American troop involvement in Vietnam escalated, so did opposition to the war among Americans at home. At first, protests against the Vietnam War were local, and relatively small. By December 1964, however, a national protest was growing. By 1965, several protests drew between ten thousand and seventeen thousand people each. In October 1967, fifty thousand people attended a single demonstration at the Pentagon.

Protesters

Many of the protesters were followers of the New Left, for whom America's involvement in Vietnam was merely a reflection of

As the war in Vietnam dragged on and mounting casualty lists were broadcast on television each night, more and more people took to the streets to protest U.S. involvement in Southeast Asia.

what they saw as their country's historically imperialist policies, by which it exploited poor countries around the world for its own economic benefit.

The biggest antiwar protest of all came in 1969, when 250,000 people crowded onto the Mall in Washington, D.C.—roughly half as many Americans as there were in Vietnam at that time.

Student Protests

Most of the protests were centered on college campuses. Although the SDS helped to organize many campus protests, the majority of the protesters had no broad political agenda. They just hated the Vietnam War and the military draft that supported it.

Student strikes temporarily shut down several colleges across the country. School administration offices were occupied by students at Columbia University in New York and the University of Wisconsin, among many others.

Faculties, as well as student bodies, were divided over the Vietnam War. While many faculty members supported the war and were outraged by the student protests

that disrupted the traditional patterns of school life, others wholeheartedly supported the protesters. There were "teach-ins" at Wisconsin and other universities, during which, instead of teaching their usual classes, antiwar faculty members lectured about the evils of colonialism and the history of American involvement in Vietnam.

Although the Vietnam War was the main source and subject of student protest, it was far from the only one. Students across the country were feeling empowered and increasingly determined to take more control of the educational experience. The Free Speech movement at the University of California at Berkeley, led by a firebrand activist named Mario Savio, demanded the right of students to speak however they wanted, including the use of four-letter words. African American students on many campuses demanded black studies classes and departments; female students demanded women's studies. Female students from Barnard held a "sleep-in" in the male dorms at Columbia University to demand that university dorms, which had always been segregated by sex, be made coed. But the largest and most disruptive protests were focused on the Vietnam War.

At times, it seemed that many American college and university campuses were little more than hotbeds of protest. And yet, as commentator Roger Rosenblatt, who was then a young faculty member at Harvard, has pointed out, "It was not an unremitting atmosphere of protest"[53]—even on the most political of campuses. Student life went on much as usual. Most students continued to attend classes, and protests were rarely very successful on fall weekends, when the majority of students were more concerned with football than with the fighting in Vietnam.

Response to the Protests

Campus authorities tolerated some protests, but eventually even the most tolerant administrations lost patience. Disciplinary actions were taken against students, and, sometimes, local police were invited onto campus to impose order.

Many students were disillusioned by the punitive reactions of their administrations. They had always considered the campus a safe place, where protest would be understood, respected, and even welcomed. Even more importantly, they had considered themselves, as students, to be highly valued members of the campus community. Now, they were amazed to find that school authorities were determined to put down the protests at almost any cost to the student participants. As Rosenblatt has said of the reaction of students at his university, they were shocked "to find that Harvard didn't care for them."[54]

At many schools, demonstrators found themselves confronted not only by members of the local police but also by armed National Guard troops, called out by alarmed state governors. Although by 1970 U.S. strength in Vietnam was reduced by 400,000, these confrontations finally bore predictable fruit when National Guard troops opened fire on student protesters at Kent State University in Ohio. Four students

In 1970 Ohio National Guardsmen fired into a crowd of student war protesters at Kent State University. Here, one of the four victims lies face down while those around him struggle to make sense of the killings.

were killed, some of whom were not even involved in the demonstrations; they had merely paused in their walk across campus, to see what was happening.

The Draft

Much of the fuel for the antiwar movement came from the opposition to the military draft. In the 1960s, as now, young men had to register with the Selective Service when they turned eighteen. Unlike now, a number of registered young men would be drafted every month, and required by law to enter the military. The number drafted varied depending on the military's needs.

The need, and the number of men drafted, went up as American involvement in Vietnam increased. And, as the numbers of draftees increased, so did the numbers of those seeking to stay out of the draft.

Hundreds of thousands of young men took steps to keep from being sent to Vietnam. They received deferments, became conscientious objectors, or dodged the draft by going underground. Some draft resisters openly defied the draft and went to jail.

Among them was the popular heavyweight boxing champion, Muhammad Ali, who refused to be inducted into the armed services in 1967. Ali, who had joined the Nation of Islam, had religious reasons for refusing to participate in the war, but he expressed them in a blunt manner that made his political position clear: "I ain't got no quarrel with them Viet Congs."[55]

His position endeared him to many anti-Vietnam activists, but it outraged the authorities. He was stripped of his heavyweight title for several years, charged and convicted of defying the draft, and sentenced to five years in prison. The conviction was later overturned.

Some sixty-eight thousand young Americans moved to Canada during the war.

Protesters burn draft cards in defiance of the Vietnam War.

Canada had no military draft and would not extradite people accused of breaking draft laws. Some of these men were draft dodgers, but others were evaders who were never actually called up for service.

The End of a Dream

For Johnson, the worst casualty of the Vietnam War was his beloved Great Society. He would later tell his biographer, Doris Kearns:

> [I] knew from the start that I was bound to be crucified either way I moved. If I left the woman I really loved—the Great Society—in order to get involved with that bitch of a war on the other side of the world, then I would lose everything at home. All my programs. All my hopes to feed the hungry and shelter the homeless. All my dreams.[56]

Yet, he felt helpless to do anything but continue the war. He could not, he felt, let the communists win in Vietnam. He could not let the dominoes fall in Southeast Asia. He could not be the first U.S. president to lose a war.

Caught between the "woman [he] really loved" and the war he felt bound to fight, Johnson tried to achieve both. "Time may require further sacrifices," he told a joint session of Congress. "If so, we will make them . . . [but] I believe we can continue the Great Society while we fight in Vietnam."[57]

He was wrong. The controversy over Vietnam destroyed his presidency, and it destroyed his dream of a Great Society. He entered the Democratic primaries as the first step in running for reelection in 1968. He won the first of the primaries against a challenge from an antiwar senator from Minnesota, Eugene McCarthy, but McCarthy did much better than he had expected.

Johnson believed in consensus. He felt that a political leader's job was to convince the various elements of the nation to work together toward a common goal. For a while he had brilliantly succeeded in doing that on the issues of civil rights and the Great Society. But he could not find any kind of consensus on the Vietnam War.

Now, he realized, the controversy over Vietnam was destroying consensus on virtually every issue. Running for reelection would divide not only the country but also his own party. He could end up losing the White House for the Democrats, losing the Vietnam War, and losing his beloved Great Society—all at once.

In a desperate effort to head off this disaster, he went on television to make a dramatic announcement:

> Fifty-two months and ten days ago, in a moment of tragedy and trauma, the duties of this office fell upon me. I asked then for your help and God's, that we might continue America on its course. . . . United we have kept that commitment. . . .
>
> What we won when all our people were united just must not be lost in suspicion, distrust, selfishness, and politics. . . . Believing this as I do, I have concluded that I should not permit the presidency to become involved in the partisan divisions that are developing in this political year. . . .
>
> Accordingly, I shall not seek and I will not accept the nomination of my party, for another term as your president.[58]

7 1968: Year of Turmoil and Tragedy

The decade of the 1960s seemed to reach a kind of critical peak in the election year of 1968, a year of upheaval, violence, assassination, and sweeping political change. Like pots that had been on the fire too long, all the problems and hopes of the 1960s seemed to boil over at once.

"The Promised Land"

Although he had been overshadowed in some circles by Elijah Muhammad and Huey Newton, Martin Luther King was still the best-known black leader in the United States. By 1968, he had shifted his emphasis from the battle to end legal segregation in the South—a battle that had been won—to a broader battle against prejudice and poverty in society as a whole.

The majority of black Americans were still poor in 1968, but King knew that poverty, like prejudice, was not just a black problem. It was the nation's problem. White people were poor, too. So were Latin Americans, Native Americans, and others. If poverty was to be conquered, it would have to be conquered for *all* Americans, not just some.

King was also convinced that all social evils were connected. Poverty, racial preju-dice, crime, domestic violence, and even the Vietnam War all fed on each other, making each other worse. The task of ending those evils was too big for King, or anyone, to accomplish, but he believed that it was his moral obligation to do what he could.

In April 1968, in order to address these social problems, King planned a massive "poor people's march" in Washington, D.C. However, before that, he went to Memphis, Tennessee, to help support a group of striking sanitation workers. It was a bitter strike, and there had recently been threats against King's life. "Well, I don't know what will happen now," he told the strikers.

> We've got some difficult days ahead. But it really doesn't matter to me now, because I've been to the mountaintop. . . . Like anybody, I would like to live a long life. Longevity has its place. But I'm not concerned about that now. I just want to do God's will. . . . I've seen the promised land. I may not get there with you. But I want you to know to-night that we, as a people will get to the promised land. And so I'm happy tonight. I'm not worried about any-thing. I'm not fearing any man. Mine eyes have seen the glory of the coming of the Lord.[59]

Martin Luther King Jr. (second from right) stands on the balcony of a Memphis motel on April 3, 1968; the following day King would be assassinated on this very spot.

The next evening, April 4, Martin Luther King Jr. was assassinated while standing on the balcony of the Lorraine Motel in Memphis as he was talking to some friends. Police determined that the killer had fired from a back window in a flophouse across the alley. A white man, James Earl Ray, who had escaped to Great Britain, was arrested by Scotland Yard in London and extradited to the United States to stand trial for the crime. At first Ray denied he was the killer, then he pled guilty and finally recanted his confession. He was, however, sentenced to life in prison. Nearly three decades later, reportedly dying, Ray was still proclaiming his innocence.

In the wake of King's assassination, new riots broke out in 168 towns and cities across the country. More than forty people were killed. *Time* magazine journalists counted over 5,000 fires, nearly 2,000 homes and stores destroyed, and almost 24,000 arrests. Officials in many cities reacted with restraint, unlike their response to some riots, in which they had ordered police to shoot looters. Perhaps they understood the rioters' rage. "It seems to me," said an African American psychologist, "a high policy decision was made to trade goods and appliances for human lives."[60] Even so, the upheaval in the cities was an ironically tragic memorial to a man who preached nonviolence.

Roughly 150,000 people attended King's funeral in Atlanta, Georgia. Among them was Bobby Kennedy, whose own brother, John Kennedy, had fallen to an assassin's bullet almost five years before. Before the year was out, Bobby would also be dead.

The Shooting Star of Bobby Kennedy

Robert Kennedy was the brightest star in American politics in 1968. His brother's death had left a void in the Democratic Party, and Bobby seemed the logical person to fill the vacuum. He was young, attractive, intelligent, and politically experienced. Most of all, he was a Kennedy.

Bobby had the reputation of being more hardheaded than his brother John,

Following King's assassination riots broke out in many cities and towns across the nation. More than forty people were killed in these riots, and arson destroyed many homes and businesses.

and more ruthless. People who knew them tended to feel warmth for John Kennedy, but they were inclined to fear Bobby. After President Kennedy was killed, however, much of the affection people had felt for him rubbed off on his brother. Bobby made the most of it.

At the time of President Kennedy's death, Robert Kennedy served as attorney general of the United States. Even though Lyndon Johnson did not get along with the younger Kennedy, the new president asked Bobby to stay on as attorney general. Bobby agreed, but resigned the next year to run for the Senate from New York. He won.

Many Democrats hoped that Bobby would run for president in 1968. Angry with Lyndon B. Johnson for escalating the Vietnam War, they thought Kennedy would be the perfect Democrat to challenge the president's renomination. They were positive that other possible anti-Vietnam candidates would alienate old-line Democratic Party leaders, but Bobby might be able to carry the banner for the antiwar forces, and hold the loyalty of traditional Democrats at the same time.

Robert Kennedy was reluctant to run so soon, however. It would not be easy to wrest the nomination from a sitting president. If he tried, it would certainly upset some important party leaders, and it might lose him their support in the future. He was still young, and better chances would probably arise in the future. When Senator Eugene McCarthy of Minnesota did well as an antiwar candidate in the Democratic primary in New Hampshire, however, Bobby knew Johnson was vulnerable; he jumped into the race.

Within days, Johnson had withdrawn his candidacy and the Democratic presidential nomination was up for grabs. Vice President Hubert H. Humphrey was the choice of most of the Johnson supporters and others who supported American involvement in Vietnam. The anti-Vietnam Democrats were split between McCarthy and Kennedy.

Each of the anti-Humphrey factions was bitter toward the other. McCarthy's supporters resented Kennedy for stealing their candidate's antiwar thunder. Kennedy's supporters argued that he was the strongest anti-Vietnam candidate and insisted that McCarthy should withdraw in order to unite the anti-Humphrey forces.

Kennedy beat McCarthy in the first three primaries he entered. (Humphrey, who had loyally supported Johnson, had not entered the primaries.) But then, McCarthy upset Kennedy in the Oregon primary, and the contest between the two anti-Vietnam candidates for the presidential nomination was back in doubt.

The last primaries were held on June 6. The biggest was in California; it was expected to be close. The winner would emerge as the leading candidate of the anti-Humphrey, anti-Johnson, anti-Vietnam forces at the party's convention in Chicago in August.

Following in his brother's footsteps, Robert Kennedy ran for president in 1968.

That night, when it became clear that Kennedy had won, the victor spoke to a crowd of his supporters in a meeting room of the Ambassador Hotel in Los Angeles. Walking to another room to speak to the press, he was making his way through a hotel serving kitchen, surrounded by friends, campaign workers, and journalists, when a young man stepped up behind him and fired a small pistol at his head.

The gunman was quickly subdued by Kennedy supporters—among them the football player Roosevelt "Rosie" Grier and Olympic athlete Rafer Johnson—but not before six people in the crowd had been shot. All the victims except the candidate eventually recovered. Robert Kennedy died a little more than twenty-four hours later in a Los Angeles hospital. The killer was a young Jordanian named Sirhan Sirhan; he was angry at Kennedy's pro-Israel political stand.

Kennedy's career as a presidential candidate had been like a shooting star. It flared up in March 1968 and soared to a decisive lead in the June primaries, only to flicker out in a burst of gunfire in the steamy kitchen of a Los Angeles hotel five months after it had begun.

Chicago

Kennedy's entrance into the race had badly split the anti-Vietnam wing of the Democratic Party. His death devastated it. Many Kennedy supporters had been devoted either to the man personally or to the memory of his dead brother. They could not bring themselves to support his rival, Eugene McCarthy. Whatever else happened at the Democratic convention in Chicago, it was clear that Hubert H. Humphrey would emerge as the presidential nominee.

Chicago was a Democratic city. In an age when many cities were slipping into decay, Chicago bragged that it was the City That Works. The man who made it work was the only really powerful political boss left in the country, Mayor Richard Daley.

Daley had dreamed of bringing the Democratic convention to his city. He knew it would focus the eyes of the nation on Chicago. He looked forward to the chance to show off his beloved city—and his own political leadership—to the world. But Daley had not reckoned on the controversy over Vietnam. He had not realized that bitterness over the war would center on the Democratic Party, on its likely nominee Hubert Humphrey, and on the Democratic convention.

He soon found out.

The mayor was outraged when antiwar protesters announced that they would descend on Chicago. He announced that no disorder would be tolerated. To back up his threat, he not only put the city's entire police force on extra duty, but he also summoned more than five thousand National Guard troops to help keep order. Thousands more regular U.S. Army troops were kept available near the city, just in case.

In effect, the mayor was warning the demonstrators to stay out of his town. Some of them did, but others took the warning as a challenge; they flocked to Chicago.

Riot police gather outside the Democratic National Convention in Chicago, preparing to quell protesters.

Looking for Trouble

There were signs that many of the protesters coming to Chicago were looking for trouble. Would-be demonstrators talked a lot about revolution and taking to the streets. Who knew when they might try to put their militant talk into action? There were wild rumors that protesters were planning to dump LSD into the Chicago water supply and "turn on" the city. Long before the convention Mayor Daley made clear that, if the protesters wanted trouble, he and his police force were ready to give it to them.

The authorities had real reason for concern. Although most antiwar demonstrations were planned to be nonviolent, they sometimes did get out of hand. It was not unknown for demonstrators to abuse police, to call them "pigs" and "fascists," or to throw rocks or other objects at them.

A federal government investigation would later describe the protesters, who actually came to Chicago as a mixed bag of "violent revolutionaries, pro-Peking sympathizers, Communists, anarchists, militant extremists, as well as pacifists, poor people's campaigners, civil rights workers . . . moderate left-wingers . . . [and] hippies."[61] Not only were there peace activists, committed to the ideals of Mahatma Gandhi and Henry David Thoreau, carrying signs that read "Suppose They Gave a War, and Nobody Came?" and "War Is Not Healthy for Children and Other Living Things," but there were also would-be revolutionaries, itching for a fight.

The Yippies

The most colorful and imaginative of the protesters were the Yippies. The high point of their stay in Chicago was their nomination of a swine they named Pigasus for president.

Many of the protesters camped out in the city's parks. "They spread their sheets upon the ground," sang the protest singer Phil Ochs, "just like a wandering tribe."[62]

The largest demonstrations were centered around Grant Park, across the street from the Conrad Hilton Hotel, where many of the delegates and candidates were staying. On the night Hubert Humphrey was nominated, the protesters tried to march from Grant Park to the convention hall. They were met, however, by a force of club-wielding Chicago police. Several of the police and roughly one thousand of the protesters were injured in the resulting confrontation. Over six hundred of the protesters were arrested.

The demonstrators were not the only ones attacked. Newspeople, including still photographers and television cameramen, were also beaten. Even inside the convention hall, some newsmen were roughed up by security forces, who were apparently outraged at what they saw as the media's negative coverage of the convention. Television, they had heard, was more concerned with what was happening in the streets than with the party's presidential nomination.

"Thousands of young people are being beaten on the streets of Chicago!" Don Peterson, the outraged head of the Wisconsin delegation, informed his fellow delegates. "I move this convention be adjourned for two weeks and moved to another city."[63]

Many Americans were appalled at the violence they saw on their television sets, violence that seemed to come primarily from the Chicago police. Among those who were most outraged were many of the anti-Vietnam delegates to the convention. Also offended was the anti-Vietnam candidate, Senator Eugene McCarthy, who had seen some of the violence from his window in the Conrad Hilton. On the last day of the convention, McCarthy visited the remaining protesters in Grant Park. "I am happy to be here," he told them, "to address the government in exile."[64]

The Chicago Eight

In the aftermath of the convention, eight of the protesters were indicted for violating the antiriot clause of the Civil Rights Act. They were charged with various criminal offenses, the worst of which was conspiring to incite a riot. Dubbed the Chicago Eight by the press, they included Yippie spokesmen Abbie Hoffman and Jerry Rubin, as well as Tom Hayden of SDS, David Dellinger, Bobby Seale of the Black Panthers, Rennie Davis, John Froines, and Lee Weiner. Like the mass of the demonstrators, they were a mixed group of New Leftists, Yippies, and pacifists. As they delighted in pointing out, they were unlikely to agree on anything, much less to unite in a conspiracy.

The Chicago Eight conspiracy trial was held in Chicago in 1969, before a crotchety judge named Julius Hoffman. The judge took some pleasure in announcing he was not related to the defendant Abbie Hoffman. The defendants were represented by the famous civil rights attorney William Kunstler and a young lawyer named Leonard Weinglass.

The defendants used their highly publicized trial as a stage for expressing their revolutionary ideals. They deliberately an-

Abbie Hoffman, one of the Chicago Eight, parades into the courtroom after being charged with inciting the riots outside the Democratic National Convention.

tagonized the judge—who needed little encouragement to demonstrate his hostility toward them. Their belief that Hoffman's courtroom was racist seemed to be proved when Seale, the only black defendant, was chained and gagged for refusing to obey the judge's order to be quiet. The Chicago Eight became the Chicago Seven when Seale was removed for a separate trial.

Although the defendants were tried for inciting a riot at the 1968 Democratic National Convention, five of the seven were eventually convicted of the lesser offense of crossing state lines with the *intent* to incite a riot. Even their lawyers were sentenced to several years by the judge, who had been outraged by their boisterous behavior in the courtroom. All the convictions were eventually overturned on appeal.

A Police Riot

The federal government commissioned Dan Walker, who would later be elected governor of Illinois, to head an investigation into the mayhem on the streets of Chicago. The Chicago authorities insisted that the demonstrators were entirely to blame, and that the police had acted with good sense and restraint. As seen by these excerpts, published in a retrospective report in the Chicago Tribune, *August 25, 1996, the Walker Report reached a different conclusion.*

"The Old Town area near Lincoln Park was a scene of police ferocity exceeding that shown on television. . . . From Sunday night through Tuesday night, incidents of intense and indiscriminate violence occurred in the streets after police had swept the park clear of demonstrators. . . . [The] violence was made all the more shocking by the fact that it was often inflicted upon persons who had broken no law, disobeyed no order, made no threat. . . .

Demonstrators attacked too. And they posed difficult problems for police as they persisted in marching through the streets, blocking traffic and intersections. But it was the police who forced them out of the park and into the neighborhood. And on the part of the police there was enough wild club swinging, enough cries of hatred, enough gratuitous beating to make the conclusion inescapable that individual policemen, and lots of them, committed violent acts far in excess of the requisite force for crowd dispersal or arrest. To read dispassionately the hundreds of statements describing firsthand the events of Sunday and Monday nights is to become convinced of what can only be called a police riot."

Many Americans viewed the police officers involved in the Chicago riots as well-armed bullies who beat and terrorized innocent young people.

My Lai Massacre

The conspiracy trial of the Chicago Seven was almost comic relief in a tragic year. The most tragic event of all that year took place half a world away from Chicago in a small South Vietnamese village known as My Lai. On March 16, 1968, the men of Charlie Company, of the U.S. Army, arrived at My Lai, which they had been told was a communist stronghold. Instead of the Vietcong soldiers they had expected to find there, they found a village filled with children, women, and old men. Angered and frustrated, they ruthlessly killed approximately two hundred Vietnamese villagers, including scores of infants and toddlers.

The massacre was kept secret for about one year. Eventually when the news reached the United States, Americans were stunned. This was the kind of thing that Americans associated with foreigners—with Nazis, communists, or barbarians of the distant past—not with Americans. And yet, the soldiers at My Lai were America's own children, not so very different from their brothers and sisters in the streets of Chicago.

A U.S. Army report on the massacre emphasized that Charlie Company was typical of young Americans. When they walked into that distant village, the military investigators reported, "they brought with them the diverse traits, prejudices and attitudes typical of the various regions of the country and segments of society from which they came."[65]

How could these Americans do such terrible things? Certainly, they were hot, angry, and sick of war. Certainly, they believed that the village was filled with communist sympathizers. But none of those things was an excuse for killing elderly women and defenseless old men, much less infants and children.

One of the participants, an ordinary young man from the Middle West named Meadlo, was interviewed on CBS by TV journalist Mike Wallace:

> Meadlo: Why did I do it? Because I felt like I was ordered to do it, and it seemed like that at the time I felt like I was doing the right thing. . . . So after I done it I felt good but later on that day it was getting to me.
>
> Wallace: You're married?
>
> Meadlo: Right.
>
> Wallace: Children?
>
> Meadlo: Two.
>
> Wallace: How old?
>
> Meadlo: The boy is two-and-a-half, and the little girl is a year-and-a-half.
>
> Wallace: Well . . . the father of two little kids like that . . . how can he shoot babies?
>
> Meadlo: I didn't have the little girl, I just had the little boy at the time.
>
> Wallace: How do you shoot babies?
>
> Meadlo: I don't know. It's just one of them things.[66]

Along with the other tragic events of 1968—including the assassinations of Martin Luther King Jr. and Robert Kennedy, and the riots in the streets of many cities—My Lai led many Americans to take a new look at themselves and their country. They could not be happy with what they saw.

Republican Victory

The Democratic Party had dominated the federal government throughout the 1960s.

Most of the great political battles of the decade had been carried out within the Democratic Party.

Southern Democrats had led the defense of segregation. Yet it had been two Democratic presidents, Kennedy and Johnson, who presided over the death of the Jim Crow laws.

The Democrats were a war party and a peace party at the same time. John F.

An Official Report on the My Lai Massacre

William R. Peers was given the unpleasant job of inquiring into the My Lai massacre on behalf of the U.S. Army. In his summary report, he described the events of March 16, 1968, as they were relayed to him by U.S. Army personnel. The report is contained in The My Lai Massacre and Its Cover-Up: Beyond the Reach of Law?, *written by Joseph Goldstein, Burke Marshall, and Jack Schwartz. In this official report the site is designated as My Lai (4), denoting that the killing actually took place in the fourth subhamlet (section) of the larger community of My Lai. As horrifying as the following account is, estimates by other investigators place the numbers of Vietnamese killed by the members of Charlie Company twice as high as the ones given here.*

"The infantry assault on My Lai (4) began a few minutes before 0800 hours [8 A.M.]. During the 1st Platoon's movement through the southern half of the subhamlet, its members were involved in widespread killing of Vietnamese inhabitants (comprised almost exclusively of old men, women, and children) and also in property destruction. Most of the inhabitants who were not killed immediately were rounded up into two groups. The first group, consisting of about 70–80 Vietnamese, was taken to a large ditch east of My Lai (4) and later shot. A second group, consisting of 20–50 Vietnamese, was taken south of the hamlet and shot there on a trail. Similar killings of smaller groups took place within the subhamlet.

Members of the 2nd Platoon killed at least 60–70 Vietnamese men, women, and children, as they swept through the northern half of My Lai (4) and through Bin Tay, a small subhamlet about 400 meters north of My Lai (4). They also committed several rapes.

The 3rd Platoon . . . followed behind the 1st and 2nd and burned and destroyed what remained of the houses in My Lai (4) and killed most of the remaining livestock. Its members also rounded up and killed a group of 7–12 women and children.

By the time [Charlie Company] departed My Lai (4) in the early afternoon . . . its members had killed at least 175–200 Vietnamese men, women, and children. The evidence indicates that only 3 or 4 were confirmed as [enemy] Viet Cong. . . . One man from the company was reported as wounded from the accidental discharge of his weapon."

Kennedy had been elected in 1960 charging the Republicans with neglecting national defense; and, although American involvement in Vietnam had begun under Dwight Eisenhower, by the late 1960s, the Vietnam War was regarded as a war fostered by the Democrats.

Lyndon B. Johnson had been the "peace" candidate in 1964—but Lyndon B. Johnson had also been the president who escalated the Vietnam War to new levels. When asked to choose between a military buildup and expanding social programs, President Johnson had chosen to do both.

In the presidential primaries of 1968, most of the national attention was focused on the Democrats. They were the party that seemed to represent, within their own party, virtually all sides of the major issues of the time. The Republicans seemed almost irrelevant. Yet, this Democratic decade would end with a Republican president. Ironically, the winner of the last presidential election of the decade was none other than Richard Nixon, the man who had lost the first to John F. Kennedy.

Nixon's victory was as much a turning point as his defeat had been eight years earlier. Before 1968, Democrats had won seven out of the previous nine elections. Republicans would win four out of the next five. For good or for bad, the decade of the 1960s had belonged primarily to the Democrats. For good or for bad, the next two decades would belong primarily to the Republicans.

Epilogue

Aftermath of a Stormy Decade

The events of the 1960s have continued to echo throughout American history, all the way down to the present. There are some lingering effects to that stormy decade.

The Counterculture

Of all the elements that made up the 1960s, the counterculture may be the one that has had the most obvious effect on American life. The way Americans dress and talk today, the music they enjoy, the drug problems that haunt many of them, and the distrust of government that affects the way they vote—all these things they inherited from the 1960s.

As Jon Margolis wrote in the *Chicago Tribune*, "The New Left may have faded away, but the counterculture did not. It became the culture."[67]

The Ongoing Conflict with Cuba

The captured survivors of the botched invasion of the Bay of Pigs were eventually ransomed for food, medicines, and farm machinery. Returned to the United States,

A young woman sits in the aftermath of a music festival. Music and fashion are just two of the legacies of the counterculture and youth movements of the 1960s.

they and other Cuban exiles continued to work for the overthrow of Fidel Castro.

Several of the exiles also continued to work with members of the American CIA, both officially and unofficially. In that role, they took part in two of the most notorious clandestine political operations that have come to light in the past several decades. Veterans of the Bay of Pigs took part in the Watergate break-in in 1972, as well as in the secret arms transfers known as the Iran-Contra scandal in 1986.

The Cuban exile community as a whole has played a major role in the growth and development of Miami and the South Florida region. In some respects, it has been said that Miami has become as much a Cuban city as an American one. The exiles have also had a significant effect on U.S. foreign policy, pressuring the government to continue to punish the Castro regime.

The Civil Rights Movement

The civil rights movement of the 1960s ended legal segregation, but failed to end racial discrimination. It did, however, ignite the pride and ambition of African Americans, and called the attention of white America to their cause. In doing so, it brought the United States a long way in the direction of racial equality.

Many of the most important changes that the civil rights movement brought about were economic and political, as well as social. According to Thomas Sowell in his book *Ethnic America:*

> Beginning in the mid-1960s . . . there were a number of areas in which blacks not only rose, but rose at a faster rate

than whites. Between 1961 and 1971, white family income rose by 55 percent. The proportion of college age young people who actually enrolled in college remained the same for whites between 1965 and 1972, but the proportion among blacks nearly doubled. The number of whites in professional-level occupations increased by about one-fifth between 1960 and 1972, while the number of blacks in such occupations nearly doubled. The number of black foremen, craftsmen, and policemen more than doubled, and the number of black engineers tripled. The number of blacks in Congress doubled between 1964 and 1972. So did the number of blacks in state legislatures around the country. In the South, the number of blacks in state legislatures more than quadrupled.[68]

Even more importantly, the civil rights movement achieved its most vital goal. It killed the Jim Crow laws. It made racial segregation illegal in the United States and destroyed the legal chains that had held millions of blacks in a new form of slavery, a century after the war to end slavery had been won.

It still has a long way to go before real equality between the races can be achieved, however. In some respects, it has moved backward in recent years. A strong political backlash has set in against many of the government programs and private measures that have helped African Americans enter the mainstream of American education and business. What is more, even many African Americans have lost faith in the ideal of more or less total integration, which inspired so much of the civil rights movement.

The civil rights movement won important victories during the volatile years of the 1960s, including the end of Jim Crow laws.

Even so, they are much closer to the ideal of integration—and to the goal of social and economic equality—than when the 1960s began.

The End of the Cold War

When President Kennedy visited the Berlin Wall in 1963, he looked forward to the day when the divided city would "be joined as one." That day finally came on the stroke of midnight, November 9, 1989. At that historic moment, the Berlin Wall was opened to the free passage of anyone who wanted to cross between the two parts of the city. The same year saw the collapse of the Soviet Union, and of the Eastern bloc that depended on it. The Cold War was over; the United States and its allies had won.

The Space Program

Speaking to the United Nations in 1961, President John F. Kennedy called for the nations of the world to cooperate in the peaceful use of outer space. "The cold reaches of the universe must not become the new arena of an even colder war."[69] At the time, that suggestion was rejected. In more recent years, there has been an increasing amount of international cooperation in space—including joint flights between the old enemies, the United States and the Soviet Union, even before the USSR was dissolved after 1989.

Although the U.S. space program has never regained the kind of national commitment it enjoyed in the 1960s, it has continued to achieve remarkable successes, particularly in the field of satellite technology. Building on the developments of the 1960s, satellites have helped to explore the earth. They have greatly increased knowledge of the weather, agriculture, and geology in particular.

Satellite technology has also revolutionized communications, to the point where television pictures can now be transmitted instantly, from virtually any place on earth (as well as from distant space) to virtually anywhere else.

Actual manned exploration of the Apollo kind has been largely abandoned, however, in favor of unmanned probes to the planets and beyond. Work has continued, however, on the development of the space shuttles that will be needed if and when manned exploration is resumed.

Assassinations

The gunmen who killed President John F. Kennedy, Martin Luther King Jr., and Robert F. Kennedy were all caught. It was hard, however, for many people to believe that these killers acted alone. Of the three, the killing of Bobby Kennedy seemed the most straightforward. Conspiracy theories about the others abounded for many years after the assassinations.

"I Just Wouldn't Have Believed It"

Was the civil rights movement a success or a failure? Perhaps the best judgment came from a black man who lived through those days in the Deep South, and who saw the changes they brought about. His name was Hartman Turnbow, and he was interviewed by the journalist Howell Raines for his 1977 book, "My Soul Is Rested": The Movement Days in the Deep South Remembered.

"Anybody hada just told me 'fore it happened that conditions would make this much change between the white and the black in Holmes County here where I live, why I'da just said, 'You're lyin'. It won't happen.' I just wouldn't have believed it. I didn't dream of it. I didn't see no way. But it got to workin' just like the citizenship class teacher told us—that if we would redish [register] to vote and just stick with it. He says it's gon' be some difficults. He told us that when we started. We was looking for it. He says we gon' have difficults, gon' have troubles. Folks gon' lose their homes, folks gon' lose their lives, peoples gon' lose all their money, and just like he said, all of that happened. He didn't miss it. He hit it ka-dap on the head, and it's workin' now. It won't never go back where it was."

The Mir space station is yet another landmark in the history of space exploration. The race to improve space technology during the 1960s resulted in the innovations that make modern space ventures possible.

Many of the theories surrounding the assassination of President Kennedy involve a Cuban connection that goes beyond Oswald's involvement in the Fair Play for Cuba Committee. It was thought that the assassination might have been ordered in Cuba, as revenge for American efforts to assassinate Fidel Castro, or that it might have been prompted by the anger of the CIA or of anti-Castro Cubans over Kennedy's restraint at the Bay of Pigs.

The killing of a civil rights leader by a white assassin was not an unusual event in the 1960s, but James Earl Ray had not acted like a typical lone assassin. He had fled the country, going first to Canada, and then to Portugal and to England, where he was arrested. This seemed more like the escape route of a contract killer, and many black Americans remain convinced that some other person or group ordered King's assassination. A congressional committee, which looked into the King assassination, reached the same conclusion, although it could not determine who else was involved.

The 1968 Democratic Convention

As a result of the events leading up to and during the Chicago convention of 1968, the Democratic Party reformed many of its rules. Political bosses like Mayor Daley have all but disappeared. Conventions are much less important today, when almost all the delegates are chosen by voters in the primaries.

Before 1968, Chicago had been a popular site for national political conventions. It would be nearly thirty years before another one would be held there. The Democrats finally returned in 1996, when they held a very different kind of carefully controlled and scripted convention to renominate President Bill Clinton for a second term.

Some political experts believe that the chaos in Chicago led to the victory of Richard M. Nixon in the November 1968 election and ushered in a new era of Republican presidents. Among those who feel that way, opinion is divided over whether the demonstrators, the police, or the mayor of Chicago were more responsible.

Others say that the split within the Democratic Party was already too deep, even before the explosion in Chicago, for a Democrat to win in November. They are convinced that, without the unified support of his party, Hubert Humphrey would have lost even if the convention had gone smoothly.

Vietnam

In the election campaign of 1968, Richard Nixon indicated that he planned to end the Vietnam War. Many Americans hoped that meant he would negotiate a quick and early end to the conflict. Privately, however, Nixon was proclaiming that "I will not be the first president of the United States to lose a war."[70] And so the Vietnam War would go on for years after the decade of the 1960s was over. The last American troops did not pull out of Vietnam until 1973, making Vietnam the longest war in U.S. history.

Soon after the Americans left, North Vietnam overran South Vietnam.

Many of those who took part in the antiwar movement of the 1960s were convinced that they and their fellow protesters ended the war. Others disagree. If anything, they say, the protests prolonged the war by giving the North Vietnamese hope that the opposition to the war at home would force the United States to pull out of Vietnam—as eventually did happen. There is no way to really know what would have happened if the protests had not taken place.

The Vietnam War greatly increased the power of American presidents to make war without asking the U.S. Congress to declare war—their constitutional right. Vietnam was the first major foreign war fought without a declaration of war from Congress. Since then, American presidents have sent troops into action in several foreign lands, including the Persian Gulf.

The Vietnam War still haunts and divides American society.

Some people believe that American prisoners of war are still being held in Vietnam, although official inquiries have not produced any evidence.

In 1977, President Jimmy Carter attempted to heal some of the wounds by pardoning the Vietnam-era draft resisters, including those who had gone to Canada.

The Great Society

President Lyndon Johnson's decision not to run for reelection in 1968 came too late to save the Great Society. The presidential election was won by Richard Nixon, and the dismantling of the Great Society was begun. Johnson would compare its ending to that of a woman starving to death. "And when she dies," he would say, "I, too, will die."[71]

Lyndon Johnson died on January 22, 1973. Many elements of the Great Society have since been destroyed. Others, including Medicare and Medicaid, continue to survive him, although they have come un-

A veteran stands in front of the Vietnam War Memorial in Washington, D.C. The national division prompted by the war remains a sore point in American history.

A Sixties Radical in the Nineties

Tom Hayden, the one-time member of the SDS who had written the Port Huron Statement in 1962, eventually went on to become a member of the California state legislature. More than three decades later, he authored the following short piece on the aftermath of the 1960s for Newsweek *magazine, which appeared in the January 3, 1994, issue.*

"If there are no memorials to the '60s, at least let there be memory. We made long strides in a short time: ending segregation, reforming presidential primaries, the 18-year-old vote, the birth of the environmental and women's movements. It may have caused the Nixon reaction, but it also made Clinton-Gore possible.

Then our idealism rusted. We were better at questioning authority than replacing it. We opposed Vietnam and the cold war, but what is our foreign policy? We opposed puritanism, but mostly with a permissive tolerance that left many moral questions unresolved. It is a time of irony. The reforms we achieved mean that many of us are absorbed in the system we protested. Yet we know the system still fails to provide good work, personal meaning, sustainability. Have we become the problem? Will the young march on us? The '60s are not over."

der increasing attack since Republicans took control of the Congress in 1994. The Republicans consider the remaining Great Society programs the cornerstones of the "big government" they despise.

The First Sixties President

On January 20, 1993, William Jefferson Clinton was inaugurated as the forty-second president of the United States. Born on August 19, 1946, Clinton was the first president who had come of age during the 1960s.

In many ways, he was typical of his generation. Although he had never been a hip-pie, or seriously into drugs, he did admit to having experimented with marijuana. As a college student, he had protested the Vietnam War, and, like many thousands of other young men of the Vietnam era, he had legally avoided military service. These things were used against him by his political opponents; they made him a controversial candidate, and probably cost him a great many votes. They were not controversial enough, however, to prevent his election as president. In 1996, he became the first Democrat to be reelected to the presidency since Franklin Delano Roosevelt.

The presidential torch—passed to John F. Kennedy's generation in 1961—had finally been passed on to the generation of Woodstock and Vietnam.

Notes

Introduction: A Time of Enormous Change and Conflict

1. Charles Dickens, *A Tale of Two Cities*. New York: Bantam, 1981, p. 1.
2. Quoted in Merle Miller, *Lyndon: An Oral Biography*. New York: G. P. Putnam's Sons, 1980, p. 363.
3. William H. Chafe, "The Spirit of '68," *Chicago Tribune*, August 25, 1996.

Chapter 1: The Torch Is Passed

4. Theodore H. White, *The Making of the President 1960*. New York: Atheneum, 1961, p. 288.
5. Quoted in Theodore C. Sorensen, *Kennedy*. New York: Harper & Row, 1965, p. 167.
6. Quoted in Louis Filler, ed., *The President Speaks: From William McKinley to Lyndon B. Johnson*. New York: G. P. Putnam's Sons, 1964, p. 375.
7. William Manchester, *Portrait of a President*. Boston: Little, Brown, 1967, p. 242.

Chapter 2: Growing Up in the 1960s

8. Charles Murray and Catherine Bly Cox, *Apollo: The Race to the Moon*. New York: Simon and Schuster, 1989, p. 13.
9. Garry Wills, "The '60s Tornado of Wrath," *Newsweek*, January 3, 1994.
10. Quoted in G. Louis Heath, ed., *Vandals in the Bomb Factory: The History and Literature of the Students for a Democratic Society*. Metuchen, NJ: Scarecrow Press, 1976, p. 216
11. William O'Neill, *Coming Apart: An Informal History of America in the 1960s*. Chicago: Quadrangle, 1971, p. 252.
12. Quoted in Joe David Brown, ed., *The Hippies*. New York: Time, 1967, p. 96.
13. Quoted in Brown, *The Hippies*, p. 97.
14. Quoted in Bruce Pollock, *When the Music Mattered: Rock in the 1960s*. New York: Holt, Rinehart & Winston, 1984, p. 117.

15. Quoted in Leonard Wolf, ed., *Voices from the Love Generation*. Boston: Little, Brown, 1968, p. 210.
16. Quoted in Wolf, *Voices from the Love Generation*, p. 252.
17. Quoted in Wolf, *Voices from the Love Generation*, p. xi.
18. Quoted in Wolf, *Voices from the Love Generation*, pp. xxxiv–xxxv.

Chapter 3: The Cold War

19. Richard M. Nixon, *The Challenges We Face*. New York: McGraw-Hill, 1960, p. 141.
20. Richard N. Current, T. Harry Williams, and Frank Freidel, *American History: A Survey*. New York: Knopf, 1975, p. 750.
21. J. Ronald Oakley, *God's Country: America in the Fifties*. New York: Dembner Books, 1986, p. 369.
22. Quoted in *The Cuban Missile Crisis*, TV Ashahi/BBC/Antelope Films, 1992.
23. Quoted in Sorensen, *Kennedy*, p. 601.
24. Quoted in Sorensen, *Kennedy*, p. 704.
25. Quoted in Sorensen, *Kennedy*, p. 704.
26. Quoted in *The Cuban Missile Crisis*.
27. Quoted in *The Cuban Missile Crisis*.

Chapter 4: The Race for the Moon

28. Hugo Young, Bryan Silcock, and Peter Dunn, *Journey to Tranquillity*. Garden City, NY: Doubleday, 1970, p. 48.
29. Nixon, *The Challenges We Face*, p. 144.
30. Quoted in Sorensen, *Kennedy*, p. 526.
31. Quoted in Sorensen, *Kennedy*, p. 529.
32. Quoted in Clifton Daniel, ed., *Chronicle of the 20th Century*. Mount Kisco, NY: Chronicle, 1987, p. 959.
33. Quoted in Norman Mailer, *Of a Fire on the Moon*. Boston: Little, Brown, 1970, p. 381.

Chapter 5: The Civil Rights Movement and the Death of Jim Crow

34. Quoted in James W. Silver, *Mississippi: The Closed Society*. New York: Harcourt, Brace & World, 1964, p. 68.

35. Quoted in "On the Fringe of a Golden Era," *Time*, January 29, 1965.

36. Quoted in Current, Williams, and Freidel, *American History*, p. 580.

37. Martin Luther King Jr., *Why We Can't Wait*. New York: Harper Collins, 1964, p. 84.

38. Quoted in David J. Garrow, *Bearing the Cross: Martin Luther King, Jr., and the Southern Christian Leadership Conference*. New York: William Morrow, 1986, p. 154.

39. Quoted in Elizabeth Sunderland, ed., *Letters from Mississippi*. New York: McGraw-Hill, 1965, p. 118.

40. Sally Belfrage, *Freedom Summer*. New York: Viking, 1965, p. 55.

41. Quoted in Garrow, *Bearing the Cross*, p. 283.

42. Quoted in Warren J. Halliburton, ed., *Historic Speeches of African Americans*. New York: Franklin Watts, 1993, p. 137.

43. Quoted in Doris Kearns, *Lyndon Johnson and the American Dream*. New York: Harper & Row, 1976, p. 229.

44. Quoted in W. R. Dell, ed., *Britannica Book of the Year 1969*. Chicago: Encyclopaedia Britannica, 1969, p. 655.

Chapter 6: The Dream of the Great Society

45. Quoted in Miller, *Lyndon*, p. 376.

46. Quoted in Miller, *Lyndon*, p. 376.

47. Quoted in Miller, *Lyndon*, p. 376.

48. Quoted in Miller, *Lyndon*, p. 363.

49. Quoted in Rowland Evans and Robert Novak, *Lyndon B. Johnson: The Exercise of Power*. New York: NAL, 1966, p. 496.

50. Quoted in Miller, *Lyndon*, p. 467.

51. Quoted in Leon Friedman and Burt Neuborne, *Unquestioning Obedience to the President: The ACLU Case Against the Illegal War in Vietnam*. New York: W. W. Norton, 1972, p. 193.

52. Quoted in "Vietnam: 'We Seek No Wider War,'" *Newsweek*, August 17, 1964.

53. Roger Rosenblatt, speech given to the Harvard Education Forum at the Harvard Graduate School of Education, Cambridge, MA, April 10, 1997.

54. Rosenblatt, April 10, 1997.

55. Quoted in Daniel, *Chronicle of the 20th Century*, p. 959.

56. Quoted in Kearns, *Lyndon Johnson and the American Dream*, p. 251.

57. Quoted in Evans and Novak, *Lyndon B. Johnson*, p. 559.

58. Quoted in Miller, *Lyndon*, p. 512.

Chapter 7: 1968: Year of Turmoil and Tragedy

59. Quoted in Garrow, *Bearing the Cross*, p. 621.

60. Quoted in "Rampage and Restraint," *Time*, April 19, 1968.

61. "Aftermath of Chicago Riots: Attack and Counterattack," *U.S. News & World Report*, December 16, 1968.

62. Phil Ochs, "William Butler Yeats Visits Lincoln Park and Escapes Unscathed," *Rehearsals for Retirement*, A&M, SP 4181.

63. Quoted in "Survival at the Stockyards," *Time*, September 6, 1968.

64. Quoted in "The Government in Exile," *Time*, September 6, 1968.

65. Quoted in Michael Bilton and Kevin Sim, *Four Hours in My Lai*. New York: Viking, 1992, p. 51.

66. Quoted in Bilton and Sim, *Four Hours in My Lai*, p. 262.

Epilogue: Aftermath of a Stormy Decade

67. Jon Margolis, "The Class of '68: The Reunion Is on the Right," *Chicago Tribune*, August 25, 1996.

68. Thomas Sowell, *Ethnic America*. New York: Basic Books, 1981, p. 221.

69. Quoted in Sorensen, *Kennedy*, p. 523.

70. Quoted in Stanley Karnow, *Vietnam: A History*. New York: Viking, 1983, p. 577.

71. Quoted in Kearns, *Lyndon Johnson and the American Dream*, p. 365.

Glossary

activist: Someone who is active in a political or social cause. The members of SDS, the antiwar protesters, and the civil rights demonstrators were all activists. So were the young men and women who worked with VISTA's community action projects.

black separatism: The belief among some African Americans that they should create their own self-sufficient society, and, if possible, their own nation.

commune: A small community in which the members live together, sharing what they have. Communes became a fad among the hippies.

deferment: A status, granted by the Selective Service, that ranked a young man ineligible to be drafted, either permanently or temporarily. Deferments were often granted to college students (temporarily) and men with families.

generation: All the people of a roughly similar age. Generations are usually counted in thirty year intervals. Parents, children, and grandchildren belong to three different generations. The sixties generation refers to those who were growing up at some time in the 1960s.

generation gap: The difficulty in communication between parents and their children, brought about by a difference in their ages, attitudes, and interests.

hippie: Originally used for the most radical of the young rebels of the 1960s. It was eventually applied to any young person who was into the counterculture scene.

Jim Crow: Any laws or regulations that prohibited blacks from associating with or enjoying the same privileges as whites.

militant: An exceptionally combative person or organization, willing to fight for their beliefs.

New Left: A political movement composed of students and various radical groups who sought sweeping social and political change.

psychedelic: Refers to the use of drugs that alter the conscious mind and the hallucinations or delusions that result from them. Also used to describe the artwork and music created under the influence of such drugs.

radical: A person who advocates extreme political or social views.

SDS: Students for a Democratic Society: one of the largest and most influential protest organizations of the 1960s. Originally the youth wing of the leftist League for Industrial Democracy, it became independent around 1960 and broke up around 1970.

straight: A term used in the 1960s for anyone who accepted the traditional values of American society.

watershed: A major event that marks a dividing line between two eras. The election of 1960 was a watershed in American politics.

White Citizens Council: A group of prominent white citizens in a town or city who held power and encouraged Klansmen to keep Jim Crow regulations in effect.

For Further Reading

Michael Bilton and Kevin Sim, *Four Hours in My Lai*. New York: Viking, 1992. A brutal, shocking, and deeply disturbing account of the My Lai massacre.

Joe David Brown, ed., *The Hippies*. New York: Time, 1967. Several quick and contemporary views of the hippies.

James A. Cooney, *Think About Foreign Policy: The U.S. and the World*. New York: Walker, 1988. Written especially for young people, it contains brief but useful sections on the Cold War, and on the effects on U.S. foreign policy in the Cuban missile crisis and the Vietnam War.

Todd Gitlin, *Years of Hope, Days of Rage*. New York: Bantam, 1989. A history focusing on the radical movements of the 1960s.

Michael Harrington, *The Other America: Poverty in the United States*. New York: Macmillan, 1962. The landmark book that awakened President John F. Kennedy—and much of the nation—to the plight of the poor in the America of the 1960s.

Martin Luther King Jr., *Stride Toward Freedom: The Montgomery Story*. New York: Harper and Brothers, 1958. King's own account of the Montgomery, Alabama, school bus boycott that served as the launching pad for the civil rights movement of the 1960s.

Julius Lester, *Look Out, Whitey! Black Power's Gon' Get Your Mama!* New York: Dial, 1968. Insights into the Black Power movement and philosophy by one of its most vocal spokesmen.

Lynda Rosen Obst, ed., *The Sixties: The Decade Remembered Now, by the People Who Lived It Then*. New York: Random House, 1977. Survivors of the 1960s look back.

Bruce Pollock, *When the Music Mattered: Rock in the 1960s*. New York: Holt, Rinehart & Winston, 1984. An enjoyable look at the music of the 1960s and what it meant to the young of the era.

Howell Raines, *"My Soul Is Rested": The Movement Days in the Deep South Remembered*. New York: G. P. Putnam's Sons, 1977. The memories of ordinary people caught up in the great struggle for civil rights, largely told in their own words.

Richard Smoke, *Think About Nuclear Arms Control*. New York: Walker, 1988. Will help young readers understand the background of the Cold War and the nuclear arms race.

John Noble Wilford, *We Reach the Moon*. Young Readers' Edition. New York: W. W. Norton, 1969. A rewriting, especially for young readers, of a *New York Times* book of the same name, telling the story of the Apollo moon mission.

Works Consulted

Books

Sally Belfrage, *Freedom Summer*. New York: Viking, 1965. An account of the black-voter registration drive in Mississippi.

Stokely Carmichael and Charles V. Hamilton, *Black Power: The Politics of Liberation in America*. New York: Random House, 1967. The views of one of the most famous spokesmen for the Black Power movement.

Michael Collins, Neil Armstrong, and Buzz Aldrin with Gene Farmer and Dora Jane Hamblin, *First on the Moon*. Boston: Little, Brown, 1970. The *Apollo 11* astronauts' own story of humankind's first voyage to the moon.

William R. Corson, *The Armies of Ignorance*. New York: Dial Press/James Wade, 1977. A largely unflattering view of the U.S. Central Intelligence Agency (CIA).

Richard N. Current, T. Harry Williams, and Frank Freidel, *American History: A Survey*. New York: Knopf, 1975. An excellent survey of American history, from the arrival of the first Europeans to the early 1970s.

Clifton Daniel, ed., *Chronicle of the 20th Century*. Mount Kisco, NY: Chronicle, 1987. The main dates and events of the first several decades of the twentieth century.

Rowland Evans and Robert Novak, *Lyndon B. Johnson: The Exercise of Power*. New York: NAL, 1966. A contemporary look at the Johnson presidency, written by two respected Washington journalists.

Louis Filler, ed., *The President Speaks: From William McKinley to Lyndon B. Johnson*. New York: G. P. Putnam's Sons, 1964. A collection of speeches and documents by twentieth-century presidents. The focus of the work is on the words that helped convey each president's public image.

Eric Foner and John Garraty, *The Reader's Companion to American History*. Boston: Houghton-Mifflin, 1991. A one-volume encyclopedia of U.S. history.

Leon Friedman and Burt Neuborne, *Unquestioning Obedience to the President: The ACLU Case Against the Illegal War in Vietnam*. New York: W. W. Norton, 1972. As its title suggests, this is an argument against the legality of U.S. involvement in the Vietnam War.

David J. Garrow, *Bearing the Cross: Martin Luther King, Jr., and the Southern Christian Leadership Conference*. New York: William Morrow, 1986. Arguably the best book on King and his role in the civil rights movement.

Joseph Goldstein, Burke Marshall, and Jack Schwartz, *The My Lai Massacre and Its Cover-Up: Beyond the Reach of Law?* New York: Free Press, 1976. A detailed examination of the massacre at My Lai and its aftermath.

Warren J. Halliburton, ed., *Historic Speeches of African Americans*. New York: Franklin Watts, 1993. A collection of speeches from African American religious leaders, politicians, and lesser-known orators. The speeches are accompanied by brief biographical sketches.

G. Louis Heath, ed., *Vandals in the Bomb Factory: The History and Literature of the Students for a Democratic Society.* Metuchen, NJ: Scarecrow Press, 1976. Contains the Port Huron Statement (the manifesto of the Students for a Democratic Society) as well as a chronology of key events in the history of the New Left during the 1960s.

Stanley Karnow, *Vietnam: A History.* New York: Viking, 1983. A comprehensive look at the war in Vietnam. Drawing on his years of experience as a journalist, Karnow fills his book with many exclusive and revealing interviews of participants on both sides of the conflict.

Doris Kearns, *Lyndon Johnson and the American Dream.* New York: Harper & Row, 1976. An account of the Johnson presidency.

Martin Luther King Jr., *Why We Can't Wait.* New York: Harper Collins, 1964. King's effort to explain African American grievances to white America.

Norman Mailer, *Of a Fire on the Moon.* Boston: Little, Brown, 1970. The author's reflections on the *Apollo 11* mission to the moon, and the men who made it possible.

William Manchester, *Portrait of a President.* Boston: Little, Brown, 1967. An admiring portrait of John F. Kennedy originally published in 1962, republished with an epilogue four years after the president's death.

Merle Miller, *Lyndon: An Oral Biography.* New York: G. P. Putnam's Sons, 1980. A biography of Lyndon B. Johnson, featuring extensive quotes from Johnson and from those who knew him.

Charles Murray and Catherine Bly Cox, *Apollo: The Race to the Moon.* New York: Simon and Schuster, 1989. An excellent account of the history and success of the Apollo program.

Richard M. Nixon, *The Challenges We Face.* New York: McGraw-Hill, 1960. A prepresidential compilation of speeches and writings reflecting Nixon's views of the issues facing the United States as it entered the 1960s.

J. Ronald Oakley, *God's Country: America in the Fifties.* New York: Dembner Books, 1986. An interesting book discussing not only the social environment that primed the 1960s, but also the beginnings of the social changes that would take place in the 1960s.

William O'Neill, *Coming Apart: An Informal History of America in the 1960s.* Chicago: Quadrangle, 1971. A readable exploration of the 1960s.

James W. Silver, *Mississippi: The Closed Society.* New York: Harcourt, Brace & World, 1964. Using the resistance to the admission of a black student to the University of Mississippi as a symbol of the state's segregation, the author provides an interesting history of Mississippi's opposition to black civil rights.

Theodore C. Sorensen, *Kennedy.* New York: Harper & Row, 1965. One of the essential biographies of John F. Kennedy, by the man who was his chief speechwriter.

Thomas Sowell, *Ethnic America.* New York: Basic Books, 1981. Sowell, a conservative African American economist, explores the histories of nine American minorities and the different ways they have adapted to life in the United States.

Elizabeth Sunderland, ed., *Letters from Mississippi.* New York: McGraw-Hill, 1965. Actual letters written by civil rights workers in Mississippi to family and friends back home.

Theodore H. White, *The Making of the President 1960.* New York: Atheneum, 1961. A respected journalist presents an inside account of both sides of the 1960 presidential campaign.

Leonard Wolf, ed., *Voices from the Love Generation.* Boston: Little, Brown, 1968. A collection of interviews of residents of the Haight district of San Francisco.

Hugo Young, Bryan Silcock, and Peter Dunn, *Journey to Tranquillity.* Garden City, NY: Doubleday, 1970. One of the most readable accounts of the Apollo program.

Periodicals and Other Sources

"Aftermath of Chicago Riots: Attack and Counterattack," *U.S. News & World Report,* December 16, 1968.

William H. Chafe, "The Spirit of '68," *Chicago Tribune,* August 25, 1996.

The Cuban Missile Crisis, TV Ashahi/BBC/Antelope Films, 1992.

"The Government in Exile," *Time,* September 6, 1968.

Jon Margolis, "The Class of '68: The Reunion Is on the Right," *Chicago Tribune,* August 25, 1996.

Phil Ochs, "William Butler Yeats Visits Lincoln Park and Escapes Unscathed," *Rehearsals for Retirement,* A&M, SP 4181.

"On the Fringe of a Golden Era," *Time,* January 29, 1965.

"Rampage and Restraint," *Time,* April 19, 1968.

"Survival at the Stockyards," *Time,* September 6, 1968.

"Vietnam: 'We Seek No Wider War,'" *Newsweek,* August 17, 1964.

Garry Wills, "The '60s Tornado of Wrath," *Newsweek,* January 3, 1994.

Index

Medicaid, 73, 98
Medicare, 73–74, 98
Mercury 3, 46
Mercury 5, 46
military draft, 26, 29,
    80–81
moon
    first man on, 51, 53
    space probes to, 45–46
Muhammad, Elijah, 67
My Lai massacre, 90

NAACP (National Associa-
    tion for the Advancement
    of Colored People), 55,
    62, 63
NASA (National Aero-
    nautics and Space
    Administration), 45,
    50, 51
National Guard, 59, 79–80,
    86
Nation of Islam, 67, 80
NATO (North Atlantic
    Treaty Organization),
    40, 43
Nixon, Richard M., 9, 33,
    46–47, 52, 97
    position on Vietnam
        War, 77, 98
    presidential candidacy
        of, 12–15, 92
NOW (National Organiza-
    tion for Women), 30
nuclear weapons, 8, 45
    see also arms race; Cuban
        Missile Crisis

Ochs, Phil, 31
Office of Economic
    Opportunity (OEO),
    72–73
Operation Mongoose, 40

Oswald, Lee Harvey, 8, 70

Parks, Rosa, 55
Peace Corps, 18
Penn, Lemuel, 63
police, 87–88, 89
Port Huron Statement, 25
poverty, 24, 82
    black, 65
    war on, 71–74
Project C, 57, 59
protests
    civil rights, 57, 59–60
    military draft, 80–81
    student, 78–80
    Vietnam War, 77–80, 98
    see also demonstrations;
        riots; sit-ins

Ray, James Earl, 83, 97
Ride, Sally K., 50
riots, 9, 66
    see also Democratic
        National Convention
rock 'n' roll, 31–32
Roosevelt, Franklin
    Delano, 16
Roosevelt, Theodore, 16
Rubin, Jerry, 88
Ruby, Jack, 8, 70

Savio, Mario, 78
Schwerner, Michael,
    62–63, 64
SCUM (Society for Cutting
    Up Men), 30
Seale, Bobby, 88
segregation, 23
sexual revolution, 27,
    30–31
Shepard, Alan B., Jr., 46
Sirhan, Sirhan, 85
sit-ins, 60–61

Social Security, 18
Southern Christian
    Leadership Conference
    (SCLC), 56, 57, 62
Soviet Union, 12, 39, 95
    relations with Cuba, 36,
        38
    see also Cuban Missile
        Crisis
    relations with U.S., 10, 33
    space exploration of, 45,
        95
space exploration, 10,
    44–53, 95–96
Spock, Benjamin, 29
Sputnik I, 45
Sputnik II, 45
Stern, Isaac, 18
Stravinsky, Igor, 18
Student Nonviolent Co-
    ordinating Committee
    (SNCC), 60–61, 62
Students for a Democratic
    Society (SDS), 25, 26, 78

television. *See* debates,
    presidential
Tereshkova, Valentina V.,
    50
Thoreau, Henry David, 56
Tonkin Gulf Resolution,
    76–77
Truman, Harry S., 16, 73,
    74
Turkey, 8
    nuclear missiles in, 40,
        43
Tuskegee Institute, 55

United Nations, 25
United States, 12
    economy of, 18–19, 24
    in 1960, 22–24

Picture Credits

About the Author

Michael Kronenwetter is a freelance writer and columnist who lives in Wausau, Wisconsin. He is the author of more than thirty books, several of which have appeared on the New York Public Library's annual lists of outstanding books for young people. Among his various titles include the books *Encyclopedia of Modern American Social Issues, Prejudice in America, The Peace Commandos, United They Hate, Protest, How to Write a News Article,* and *Journalism Ethics,* which has been translated into Japanese. This is his first book for Lucent Books.